D1096677

Poetry Ireland REVIEW 99

Eagarthóir/Editor

CAITRÍONA O'REILLY

Poetry Ireland Ltd/Éigse Éireann Teo gratefully acknowledges the assistance of The Arts Council/An Chomhairle Ealaíon and The Arts Council of Northern Ireland.

Poetry Ireland invites individuals and commercial organisations to become Friends of Poetry Ireland. For more details please contact:

Poetry Ireland Friends Scheme
Poetry Ireland
2 Proud's Lane
off St Stephen's Green
Dublin 2
Ireland

or telephone +353 1 4789974; e-mail management@poetryireland.ie

PATRONS:
Joan and Joe McBreen   ColourBooks Ltd

Poetry Ireland Review is published quarterly by Poetry Ireland Ltd. The Editor enjoys complete autonomy in the choice of material published. The contents of this publication should not be taken to reflect either the views or the policy of the publishers.

ISBN: 1-902121-37-6
ISSN: 0332-2998

ASSISTANT EDITOR: Paul Lenehan, with the assistance of Jessica Colley, Katie Holmes, Conor Leahy and David Maybury.
DESIGN: Alastair Keady (**www.hexhibit.com**)
Printed in Ireland by **ColourBooks Ltd** Baldoyle Industrial Estate Dublin 13.

Contents   Poetry Ireland Review 99

Rita Ann Higgins

THIS WAS NO ITHACA

The women of Baile Crua
never filled their heads
with yellow and pink rollers
letting on to be going somewhere
when there was no somewhere to go.

Somewhere was where other women went
women with magnolia vision
and pencil shaped dreams
and always a jezebel cigarette
between those blood-red lips.

The women of Baile Crua
filled their heads
with a loving Godling
whom they duly served
every waking second.

They implored their loving Godling
to follow their vagabond sons
down the alleyways of Cricklewood
and Camden Town and further afield.

If the pencil shapers
turned the heads of the husbands
and if the husbands called out the wrong name
when they were claiming their God-given rights,
what harm was it for God's sake.

It was fine with the women
who never filled their heads
with yellow and pink rollers
and never let on to be going somewhere
when there was no somewhere to go.

These women were busy imploring
their loving Godling
to keep their daughters in a state of grace
until the wedding night
and not allow shame to fall on the family
by any daughter of theirs waddling down the aisle
with a belly full of baby.

For the favours sought from
their loving Godling
the women with no rollers
would wear their knuckles inside out
making God's altar shine.

And God's marble was a sheet of ice
and the husbands whose heads were
pencil shaped turned
saw themselves in it when they went up
to receive the body of Christ.

The women of Baile Crua
made many sacrifices,
and the deity was always the same
their own loving Godling.
He hung out in the ether
and in the hedges
and other hiding places.

He kept them on their toes
they praised him often
at door steps with arms folded
at bus stops and at the solemn novena
and any place that resembled a cross,
ditch, *bóithrín* or bog.

Except for Missus all over Hurt
who had no deity that wasn't
in a small brown bottle
that brought instant rapture
when she tossed three or four
of them beauties onto her palm.
They took away the rasping pain

of the day, the other women's God
let her only son kiss the face of a raging truck.

This was no Ithaca
no sweat was ever broken
trying to reach here.
You could get here by taking
a bus from the Square
and collecting your parked bike
from a friend's garden
and cycling the last mile.

There was no Poseidon here
to blow a hole in your dreams
this was a place you didn't need
rollers in your hair for,
letting on to be going somewhere
when there was no somewhere to go.

This was Baile Crua
all you needed was a loving Godling
to polish and die for.

Peter Carpenter

LOCUST

Part of some crack marine crustacean airborne fleet,
shorn of antennae, mistaken for a flying lobster
by some tired Roman gauleiter on the retreat
from Africa, you are the last jigsaw puzzle piece –
with no Pythagoras to unlock you – or some low-life extra
in a leather boiler suit yomping across the stage
with his charnel house mates.
                                               Riot shield humour,
copper jaws, reinforced eggshell perspex body armour:
your crew really know how to spread the shit: famine,
havoc, death; from some thousand-plane daylight raid
you've dumped beans, birds and borers into our mouths;
compound eyes in the zone, riding a dirty hunch, clamped
until kingdom come on your partner's back, as short on social
skills as a sandstorm, you're all set for one last fucking rampage.

Peter Carpenter

TO A PIPISTRELLE

Forgive us
our early evening summer drinks,
our interference
to your fine-tuned reception, our wittering across Chardonnay,
our Stan Getz
or Arvo Pärt drifting your way with nicknames you won't get
past sonics,
our fripperies of laughter that draw you down come dusk:
full tilt Billy
Whizz, gut-curving bullet dive, liquorice sheen, an even
giggle and then
back on up to an Arts and Crafts chimney, registering an exit to light.

Róisín Tierney

GOTHIC

When the cathedral closed its walls about you,
the exit disappeared and you were forced
into a semi-run around the nave
and out into the interminable outer rooms
situated around the rotting cloister,
your hackles rose, you found yourself hard pressed
to like this tête-a-tête with *meaningful* art;
Sebastian, shot through with quivers full of arrows,
Lucia, holding her eyes out on a plate,
the effigy of a dead boy-king, his tomb,
a serpent winding round a giant sceptre,
its head a gargoyle's, its eyes a stony gaze,
the mummied finger of a forgotten saint.
The point of which, as you yourself confessed,
was lost on you. You looked up at the apse,
still running slightly, and slightly out of breath,
tripped, fell, and stifling an oath,
sprawled forward on the flags beneath the quire.
Then all went dark. Even the Gregorian chant
endlessly emanating from the round tape,
met its own death, its relative rigor mortis.
That's when the pig, you say, Iberian, *Pata Negra*,
conjured, perhaps, from the damp parts of your mind,
ambled forward and poked you with its snout,
it being a pig, and spoke to you in *English*,
though in Spanish it might have rhymed.
And you now dare to stand before this court
and maintain you can't remember all you heard,
(in spite of our inducements to the contrary)
apart from the occasional snatch of nonsense,
phrases such as '*Mind the flying buttress*'
or '*We are simple, you and I*'. Then the pig,
after a reference to '*rutting in the jungle*'
or some such other smut, winked, and gently
nudged you towards the door. On the way
it stopped and bowed to Francis, ever kind,
concerned even for the providence of birds –

as you left, it grunted softly in your ear,
'Drop in anytime, you are always welcome here.'
We find you guilty of the gravest heresy.

Jason Ranon Uri Rotstein

NO GREAT ARTIST

By now, she is well past her literary prime
But she never had one

She never retired like Bellow in his old age
Now and then, I receive one of her letters

> *I hope you are well and settling in and getting into the routine.*
> *It was so great hearing your voice yesterday like sunshine coming*
> *through the telephone.*

She still writes in longhand
On fine stationery left over from one of mom's affairs

> *I saw Mom and Dad yesterday – they were just back from Montreal*
> *and LA.*
> *The house is empty – just Sam. She will have to get used to it.*

With none of that abiding care for diction, syntax and grammar
Her style is best described informative

You ask me, she leaves Hemingway in the dust
Pushing the sentences to new extremes

> *For you it is a total new experience but a great one. We are so*
> *lucky to have*
> *enjoyed each other, the lunches, the movies, etc – just to enjoy our*
> *talks – time together.*

Unvarnished short declarative sentences
Just a free-associative string

> *I will try and mail this to-day if I can get out.*
> *Please excuse the shaky handwriting.*

Complete with cross-outs and slanting lines
But I think she manages very well in all

I love you. Look after yourself.
Will write again.

I find my grandmother's shaky cursive
                              Reads best in low light
Wherever   Painful red eyes contract.

Carrie Etter

SOLITARIES

My belly curves
(it has no fruit)

as your body, swollen
where immobile,

achieves a difficult rest.
Time stretches into

solitude, when most nurses
have gone home to

beds that cannot
rise and bend.

The motion in the tubes
is silent; the wound vac

purrs through the night.
Such is your room

without me, who, alone
if barren, am also pulse,

breath, voice, and the
distinct sound of otherness

in footfall.

Carrie Etter

BLUE COAT
after Magritte's *Pascal's Coat*

The air, heavy with rain having fallen and rain about-to-be, opaque with the indefatigable sorrow, the loiterer on the corner, at the cross-roads. Breathe.

While the bougainvillea's bright petals bear last night's rain. Morning has not come: Night persists into the sight-bound hours.

Into the plateau of abstraction, narrative goes. *Once there was a town in which everyone coveted the blue of periwinkles.*

As the sun ascends, the air gradates to lighter hues: white of day-old snow alongside a street.

Sorrow cannot be solved, and yet *once a stranger came into the town wearing a fine wool coat of just that blue.*

Do you see the blue coat rising over the town until it hovers a hundred yards over it, bearing as many holes as snatches of cloth?

The story invents its audience, to see the coat in the air, scraps of fabric in the hands of a boy, a shopkeeper, a seamstress.

And now the rain, insistent, pervades; rolls off the bougainvillea.

The shopkeeper's daughter carries a long grey coat. I carry a long grey coat as a weak apology to the stranger, the one man in the crowd who does not gaze up.

And I slide on the coat which does not quite fit, and nod thanks to the girl, and do not look up until the darkening sky fills the hovering coat's holes with another blue. Breathe, and the rain.

Carrie Etter

MELANCHOLIA

It is like a stranger, a clean-shaven man with all his teeth, asking which bus will take him to Aldwych. You know the answer, and you've been working alone all day, so you respond with detail and encouragement. The next question is personal yet a little flattering: what do you think of that book you're holding, that he's heard such things about, or do you work around here, it's such an interesting part of London. You hesitate but smile, and keep this answer to two or three sentences. How the conversation progresses from that exchange, to the story of his apparently warranted desertion by his wife of nine years and their two children, you never remember afterwards, but at last you walk away in utter weariness. After a while, you notice a dragging shoelace, but cannot bear to tie it.

Peter Robinson

FENCE PALINGS

> 'Es war einmal ein Lattenzaun...'
> – Christian Morgenstern

Fierce sun strikes my daughter's face
as she turns back to the door
and smiles, smiles, late for school;

then hurtles off around the corner...
as if between brick courses,
the cut grass patch's grass blades,
or fence palings' empty spaces
were your possibilities,
ones no architect could steal
nor councillor condemn –

and, again, I'm thinking of
interstices, the front path pebbles',
so many you could never tell
their number, number possibilities,
troubles, homework, love,
as again I'm thinking of
your welfare and farewell.

Simon Haworth

BUS SHELTER, BARROW-IN-FURNESS

The facts in logical space are the world,
the snowy owl scratching its nest on a mound
of scrap metal, and a length of unmarked road
where a generator chatters ear to the ground.
I listen to the wind alive inside an empty
blister pack, the confluence of oil spill and estuary.

Disintegrating between pale sea and sky
you catch the terminal flight of leaf and spoke,
another gift of *structural amnesia*.
We worked all day and at night our influence
in baggage handling got us half-drunk,
striking us out of human memory.

From a breaker's yard that washed-up poet
de Campos looks out to Piel Island,
oasis of Puritanism and piracy.
He studies the blueprints for a cruise liner
bristling with droplets of cloud-smelt.
These things must simply be felt.

I have spent my nights dug in like infantry
bath tub doubling as bed and water trough.
Through this material rivers seethe,
parks grow forlorn. I am dying, that is enough.
When the final bulb in the foreign embassy
goes out, there will be no one left to blame.

Simon Haworth

WAVE

The forecasters predict the harbours will boom;
in bland towns, the rain
sweeps across neglected gardens.
A commuter lies awake in a spare room.

The headlines trip over themselves to uncover
which side came off worse in the most
recent drive-by and the exact motivations
of the arrested protestor.

Light pollution
inspires new mythology on stars,
though far off, shopping centres
empty and darken.

Scaffolding clings to the multi-storeys
like ivy; in stations news breaks
across the tannoys of a further trespasser
on the West Coast main line.

Kevin Graham

DIVING

The roads were heavy with dust, dry from a sun
hot with desire. We glistened as our sun-cream

slid away. The bridge brought trucks further
up the Cape, rumbling past, sometimes hooting.

We all stripped down to our trunks above the river,
rushing coolly underneath. It was a five foot drop.

We leapt off the edge and strode through the air,
yelling to ourselves. My world changed then.

As I plumbed the river's chest, feeling fish slip
between my arms and legs, I realised our love

was over: that we had grown apart from each other.
It dawned on me you were seeing someone else.

That realisation weighed me down like a drug;
the anchor had always been planted in my dreams.

I was overcome, curiously clawing at my chest,
as if until now I had not known what it contained.

I opened my eyes and saw silt sail past, but never
any fish; I only sensed they were there, darting.

When I came up for air you were gone. My eyes
drank the sky in gulps, my breath not yet taken.

Lisa Steppe

SHARING WITH CAMUS

the muscle of an old love story,
bruised, yes. Sharing restlessness,

the colour of the shipmate's
piano, the pelt of the early

morning earth, the golden fleece
of dunes, the sea, the taut

bodhrán of combers. Sharing
doing as if we were

millstones, grinding grain,
makers of bread. Sharing

turning when we turn our heads
to see the wise horizon

of the prairie shrinking. Sharing
suffering, you hand me

the daily food of your questioning,
I give you fear. Sharing

the light with you, the light
of the southern hour

when time unfolds like a girl's
silken skirt and we celebrate

our infinite encounter and I see
myself reflected in your eyes –

I, the stranger, the cancer lady –
as a loved one.

Jim Maguire

BEFORE THE INVASION

We had lost nearly everything, father said. We would have to open the house to the public.

The tower

Through the oriel, the park
the fountain, the Great Wall
of shelterbelt oaks
weaving through the clouds

a darkening cirrus
where sky meets mountain

The coachyard

Hammer blows ringing

a café and tourist shop for the haybarn

music echoing
in the dappled corners
early summer nights
when the chain of lanterns shone...

Under the belvedere window

Father's voice asking if she can hear it
the implacable drone
the lowest note on the organ.

Mother descanting again
about the chill in her bones,
the white wolf she keeps inside

its need to be unleashed
its abhorrence of the blue pills

...They only tie a rope around it
dress it up in ridiculous clothes...

A leaf floats *sotto voce*
above the moss brocaded slates.

The millrace

A twilight practice-run
through the flitting places

the stream wandering in search
of its dried-up song

losing heart in the woodland
rallying in the darkness
of the overflow carpark.

The orchard

Stumps in the knee-high grass
wanting to shout out to the world

the millstone
rising up in the night's throat

no escape
from the encroaching hoofbeats

rows of trees with their ghoulish arms
tuned-in to a far-off grief

nettles rampant over the clearing
where mother once sat with her easel.

The reeds

The mouldering boathouse
where the snow princess sleeps

a flutter in her breathing
sending out delicate ghosts

mist clouds unscrolling
above the frozen lake

Father in his great coat
conducting Bruckner in the top field

drawing a hand through his life
always catching this slope, this light...

Under the frost the silent earth
the descending stairway to the bonfire

glow of her dream, the ecstasy of melting
among the minarets and cypresses

men in teal and tangerine
weaving their overstacked motorbikes

through narrow streets
hawkers' cries fading to a streak

in the graduated wash of the sky.

Jim Maguire

MUSIC FIELD

Then comes the bit he's been practising for years
but still can't get his hands around. The melody's
giddy unwrapping above the distressed inner parts,
the bass-line an unimpressed patriarchal yawn.
So why the end-of-world hush that falls over the hall?
As if on the cyclorama Lady Lavery as Caitlín
has stepped out of the pound into a stony field
with its single windswept tree like a headscarf.
Is it the tree she's trying to stare down or the boy
half-hidden behind in stiff breeches and spats,
outlandish get-up for a field, not to mention his hair
full of flowers – poppy, marigold, cyclamen –
a key in his head for each, all flat-majors and a minor
for the fuzzy horizon. Two unrelated themes
in a field, slow-circling, waiting for the trouble to begin.

Mick Wood

A TUESDAY

look at him
what's he doing there?
doesn't he know it's a Tuesday?

fucking idiot
what? he can't hear me
not with that thing on his head

can't even hear himself think
not with that thing on his head
fucking idiot

well let him stand there
and he'll see what he gets
and we'll see how he likes it

what? come off it
you go
if you're so bothered

I'm not going near the place
not on a Tuesday and not
with someone like him hanging around

what's he doing there?
waiting? waiting for who?
all right all right waiting for *whom*?

I don't
I don't care
I don't give a monkey's

if he wants to get himself
who waits there for someone?
would you wait there?

on a Wednesday yes
yes of course on a Wednesday
but this is a Tuesday

fucking idiot
no not you
that fucking idiot

standing there
with that thing on his head
on a Tuesday

Mick Wood

MASOCHIST

as the thigh in jodhpurs
invites bunched gloves
to slap and slap

as long boots plead
with the riding crop

as the half-drowned buoy
yearns for a stoning

as knee-high nettles yell
grab a stick
have at us!

so does my high-horsed
jack-booted
rubber-clad
poisonous
body

ache

for your correction

Maria Johnston

THE BARD OF LOVE: MICHAEL LONGLEY AT 70

'A milestone and not a headstone' is how Michael Longley described his *Collected Poems* on the occasion of its publication in 2006. Prior to that defining moment he had declared that the very mention of a *Collected Poems* 'sounds like a tombstone'. Longley's reservations about his poetry being solidified into the marmoreal opus of a *Collected Poems* bear out his long-held belief that poetry is a vital, organic process. For Longley, writing confirms life while the finished *oeuvre* signifies the opposite; the finality and fixity of death. 'Au revoir, *oeuvre!*' he has exclaimed in the face of such stultifying entombment. And so, on the occasion of Longley's seventieth birthday, it seems fitting to focus on his poetry as an open-ended and ever-enlarging site of continuity and renewal, and to look specifically at the poems that he has produced in the years since the *Collected Poems* rounded off his *oeuvre* into one magnificent, though by no means complete, tome. 'To be continued…' the provisional ending of that tome seemed to wink at the reader and we have truly entered a new phase since then. Each of the poems that Longley has published in journals and magazines since that moment seems more miraculous than the last; to happen upon a new poem by this poet between the pages of a quarterly publication or a daily newspaper is akin to discovering a rare orchid flowering in a wilderness. As Longley, now a septuagenarian, moves into the old age that was so enabling for many of the finest poets and artists – W B Yeats, Wallace Stevens and Walt Whitman come to mind first off – his words are moving more gracefully than ever.

More than anything else, Longley's recent trove of post-*Collected* poems continues to illuminate what may be termed his poetics of love. Love is, as he has elucidated in an oft-quoted remark, at the 'core of the enterprise' and, as *The Rope Makers* published in 2005 attests to, Longley is, without question, one of the century's greatest poets of love, sex and the erotic. Indeed, the most outstanding tribute to Longley in the recently published festschrift for the poet's birthday, *Love Poet, Carpenter*, was, for me, Fran Brearton's perceptive reading of Longley's love poem 'The Pattern', a poem that looks back on the poet's wedding day and is as intricately constructed as the bridal dress itself. To my mind, Longley can be seen as part of a tradition of twentieth-century Irish love poets that extends back to W B Yeats through Louis MacNeice; indeed MacNeice is a kindred poet in terms of his own poetics of love and, with his dark, death-inflected love poems such as 'The Introduction' and 'The Sunlight on the Garden', is an important precursor for Longley. The erotic yet death-shadowed ending of MacNeice's 'Mayfly' – 'But when this summer is over let us die together, / I want always to be near your breasts' – could have been penned by Longley himself, so close is it in tone to that of his own poetry.

The recent 'Cloudberries', published in the *New Yorker* in 2007, testifies to Longley as a perennial love poet in old age:

> You give me cloudberry jam from Lapland,
> Bog amber, snow-line tidbits, scrumptious
> Cloudberries sweetened slowly by the cold,
> And costly enough for cloudberry wars
> (Diplomatic wars, my dear).

This is a delicious love poem, an *amuse-bouche* that is brimming over with oral pleasures. In the first line we enjoy the full, mouthy sounds of 'jam' and the French kiss of 'Lapland'. The mouth music of these lines is made up of a profusion of soft sibilants – 'snow-line', 'scrumptious', 'sweetened slowly' – and this suggestive pattern continues into the second stanza, in words such as 'us', 'harvesters', 'distance', 'sphagnum', 'longest', and so on:

> Imagine us
> Among the harvesters, keeping our distance
> In sphagnum fields on the longest day
> When dawn and dusk like frustrated lovers
> Can kiss, legend has it, once a year. Ah,
> Kisses at our age, cloudberry kisses.

As the poem progresses, the sensuous sibilants marry with the throaty 'c' sounds (of the repeated 'cloudberry', of 'cold', 'costly, and moving into 'dusk') to form the abundant triad of delectable 'kisses' in the poem's climactic closing lines. The opening line, 'You give me', also seems to echo the opening line of one of Longley's first published poems 'Marigolds' from 1960: 'She gave him marigolds / the colour of autumn'. Such resonant echoes are everywhere in Longley's work – one needs to have a musical memory as one reads it – and it is fitting that this late love poem should call out to another that was written when Longley was a mere fledgling poet. Longley's is a complex, full-bodied music and this poem is best heard aloud delivered in all its mouthy sensuality. Furthermore it is a poem that calls for a similar love and close attention on the part of the reader, as it requires the reader to carry out some botanical studies of their own in order for its meaning to be fully savoured. The cloudberry, relatively unknown to Irish readers, is native to Northern regions, and survives harsh weather conditions in order to grow – here the cold has 'sweetened' the cloudberries – and is notoriously difficult to harvest and to cultivate. It is therefore expensive and demands great efforts of labour from those who seek it. As a result, 'cloudberry wars' ensue between rival would-be-proprietors. Thus, a gift of cloudberry jam is so rare as to be an almost-impossible miracle; it is a gift of love born out of perseverance and effort. Interestingly, the botanical name for the cloudberry derives from the Greek 'on the ground', making for a dizzying conjunction of the immensities of the earthly and the airy. Love opens up the vastness of the world in all of its polarities to the recipient; heaven and earth, dusk and dawn reconcile in a cloudberry kiss.

One cannot proceed far into Longley's poetry before coming to his beloved Carrigskeewaun; one of his 'holy places'. His love affair with the life of this secluded landscape and natural habitat has always been at the heart of his work and he has for decades lived between the two parts of Ireland that he 'loves most': Belfast and Carrigskeewaun. It was along the River Lagan that he 'fell in love with wild birds and wild flowers' as a boy, until later, as he has described: 'I fell in love with Carrigskeewaun the first time I saw it, more than thirty years ago'. 'January', not included in *Collected Poems*, is a strikingly memorable freeze-frame of this remote place:

> The townland is growing older too.
> It makes sense to be here in the cold:
> Fuchsia's flowerless carmine, willow's
> Purple besom. We are lovers still.
> Mistiness and half a moon provide
> Our soul-arena, a tawny ring.

This is a bare, uncompromising landscape, devoid of any of the trappings of human life. It is the place of souls, encircling the human lovers in an amber glow of mist and moonlight as they age with the land and feel with it the progress of time. The landscape has an austere beauty as it is captured in a heightened, ethereal quality with its fuchsia's vivid reds, and, more ghostly still, the skeletal purple willow taking on the appearance of a witch's broom set against the overcast, half-moon-lit sky. Here, as elsewhere, Longley does not need to use end-rhyme or a fixed metrical scheme to achieve his effects; the pulsating syllabic music of the lines is freer than rigid patterns of end-rhyme or metre would allow for. It is the internal chimes between words that create meaningful linkages of sound: the gaping 'o's of 'growing older' and 'cold' create an eerie atmospherics that spells absence and exposure. Both meanings of 'still' coincide to remind us of the fact of the lovers' mortality, their deathly stillness, as well as the resilience of their love in the face of that mortality. The suggestive, mysterious quality of this perfectly shaped, concise piece means that it holds the reader suspended long after the last word has sounded.

What Victor Hugo termed the 'art of being a grandfather' is central to Longley's love life, that is to say, his poetic life. Grandchildren represent the life to come. When putting together his *Collected Poems*, Longley deliberately appended two new poems to his grandchildren so as to end 'on an up-note'. 'The Fold' is a prayer for his newborn grandchild as she lies sleeping:

> Why would the ewes and their lambs
> Assemble as though hypnotised
> Around the cottage? Do they sense
> A storm on its way? Or a fox?
> Darkness and quiet are folding
> All the sheep of Carrigskeewaun,
> Their fleeces lustrous, long wool
> For a baby's comfort-blanket,
> For Catherine asleep in her crib
> This midnight, our lambing-time.

Here, S T Coleridge's 'Frost at Midnight' with its 'secret ministry of frost' comes to mind. As in Coleridge's poem, the reason behind the animals' intuitive gesture in 'The Fold' must remain one of the countless unfathomable mysteries of the natural world. It appears that the sheep of Carrigskeewaun, the mothers and their lambs, bringing with them light and heat, instinctively seek to protect and comfort the vulnerable infant from the forces of violence and disorder that surround her in this dark, noiseless environment. As so often, the poet is questioning, probing the nature of existence. Carrigskeewaun is not a 'cosy community' as Longley has explained. It is isolated, 'haunted' by the ghosts of Famine, and under threat of extinction itself. 'I want there to be peace for my grandchildren to hear the wind in the chimney,' is Longley's secular prayer in prose.

As must be already evident from the small number of poems attended to thus far, the term 'love poetry' is an extensive one for Longley and it includes far more than the easy categorisation might otherwise denote. It is, furthermore, impossible to separate his articulations into separate categories of love or death or nature or war. 'Death and sex. What else is there to write about?' Longley has quipped. Love poems, elegies, as Longley has said, are one and the same – the terms are interchangeable – and his new poems, his poems of old age, engage with the twin realities

of love and death with a sure sense of new artistic and imaginative possibilities opening up. The mode of self-elegy– evident in Longley's earlier
work such as, for instance, 'Detour' from *Gorse Fires* (1991) and in 'Above
Dooaghtry' from *Snow Water* (2004) – has been intensifying in Longley's
more recent poems. As W H Auden identified, writing is born out of
loneliness: 'Writing begins from the sense of separateness in time, of
"I'm here today, but I shall be dead tomorrow, and you will be active in
my place and how shall I speak to you?"' In this way, through the mode
of self-elegy, Longley writes from the threshold of life and death, profess-
ing love poems to this precarious world that he must one day leave behind.
In the staggering self-elegy, elegy, and, ultimately love poem, 'The Lifeboat',
published in *The Irish Times* in 2008, the poet begins by scripting the ideal
circumstances for his own death:

> I have imagined an ideal death in Charlie Gaffney's
> Pub in Louisburgh: he pulls me the pluperfect pint
> As I, at the end of the bar next the charity boxes,
> Expire on my stool, head in hand, without a murmur.

The exuberant pun on the word 'pluperfect' points up the wittiness of
Longley's poetry and he plays darkly with the present perfect tense
throughout. The poem's next stanza is an appropriately low-key
celebration of human connectedness as both men act out a last moment
of togetherness; after solving a crossword puzzle together they 'commune
with ancestral photos'. So comfortable are they in their shared silence and
so peaceful is the poet in his repose after having soundlessly breathed his
last, that Gaffney fails to notice the death until close of business. Then
comes the turn:

> But it's Charlie Gaffney
> Who has died. Charlie, how do I buy a fishing licence?
> Shall I let the dog out? Would the fire take another sod?
> The pub might as well be empty forever now. I launch
> The toy lifeboat at my elbow with an old penny.

The shock of Charlie Gaffney's death is conveyed by Longley's masterful
use of heavy enjambment. The indented position of the stanza's first line
makes for a disorientating shift, and then, as the line does a violent u-turn
over the line-break to the other side it delivers the killer blow – 'Gaffney /
Who has died' – while the irrefutable reality of death is further
underscored with an inflexible full-stop. The list of unanswered questions
that follows, each echoing into the emptiness, is heart-breaking in its
poignancy. Each question steps up the pain of loss, repeating over and

again the fact that Charlie Gaffney's necessary presence as the lifeboat that brought those in need to some safe harbour, is gone; he can no longer communicate the answers or throw out the lifeline. The 'I' is nothing without a 'you' to answer and restore it.

Longley's love poems take place between a 'you' and 'I' as the poet reaches out to another, to a reader or a listener, or to one who is absent. As Longley himself has identified: 'The "you" and "I" are like two posts holding up a clothes line'. The poems hinge on an 'I' calling out to a 'you'. Tellingly, the word 'call' recurs in his recent poems. In 'Call', published in *Poetry Review*, the speaker is preoccupied with reaching out to a friend who is elsewhere, 'alone', in a place that lies at the remotest point of human tenancy:

> Alone at Carrigskeewaun for the millennium
> My friend sits at the hearth keeping the cottage warm.
> Is it too late to phone him? Is it midnight yet?
> That could be me, a meadow pipit calling out.
> Otters are crossing from Dooaghtry to Corragaun.
> There are mallards and widgeon and teal for him to count.
> Three dolphins are passing the Carricknashinnagh shoal.
> He has kept for this evening firewood that is very old.
> Bog deal's five thousand years make the room too hot.
> How snugly the meadow pipit fits the merlin's foot.

What strikes one first about this poem is the closeness that exists between the distant poet as the speaker of the poem and his silent friend. Although the poet is far-removed from the site he seems to have a view into the cottage in Carrigskeewaun nevertheless, and is sensitively aware of his friend's movements and the movements of the world of nature at his door; the soundscape, the landscape of the townland is alive and perceptible to him even from his far-off vantage point. In order to breach the distance between them, the poet imaginatively takes the form of a familiar songbird and makes himself present as 'a meadow pipit calling out'. This phenomenon of call and response that is, in my view, so crucial to Longley's poetics, brings to mind the bird of Whitman's operatic poem 'Out of the Cradle Endlessly Rocking'; the bird has lost his mate and sings expressive, grief-laden arias – 'carols of lonesome love' – calling out to her only to meet with silence, death, in return. Whitman's 'lone singer' is the mocking-bird – not the nightingale – which reminds us of Longley's declared preference for the pipit, the blackbird, over Yeats's golden bird of Byzantium. As the awakening poet 'Listen'd long and long. / Listened to keep, to sing, now translating the notes' he becomes the 'outsetting bard of love', and it is the musical counterpoint between 'the notes of the bird continuous echoing', and the incessant moaning of the sea whispering death, that gives birth to the poet's own song: 'My own songs awaked from that hour, / And with them the key, the word up from the waves'. The Carrigskeewaun cottage was 'once a music box', as Longley has described it, alive with communal gatherings of story-telling, music-making and singing. Now it is left to the poet, to Longley as the 'bard of love', to create the music of the place as he goes on translating the songs of the birds, listening for the sounds of nature around him, and always calling out. But the inescapable ground bass of death has always been there in his work too and is nowhere more apparent than in his most recent poetry.

The poem 'Greenshank', published in *The Lake without a Name* (2005) anticipates the point of crossing over into death and considers how the poet may communicate – and commune – with his loved ones, his readers, after he has left the earth: 'When I walk from Carrigskeewaun for the last time, / I hope you discover something I overlooked'. For ultimately, despite the poet's attentive listening to and watching over Carrigskeewaun as he has explored it over the decades, his eyes and ears will have missed something in this multi-layered, multivarious and ever-changing spot. As Longley has said of Carrigskeewaun, 'I'd need several lifetimes to get to the bottom of this tiny townland.' The same deep sense of the land as a repository of history that is there in 'Call' – where the aged bog deal has survived from the ancient world and is far older than the calendar system that is being celebrated with the new millennium – is here in 'Greenshank' with its 'burial mound' as signifier of the ghosts that haunt the landscape and the ubiquitous presence of death. The question at the heart of this poem presages the unstoppable changes that will impact even on this most constant location in Longley's work: 'How long will Carrigskeewaun remain a lake?' As the poem pledges in its final lines, the call of the greenshank will remind those left behind of the poet's legacy as he bequeaths to those who will live on after him the gifts of love and attentiveness for the creatures, both human and non-human, of this fragile earth; the greenshank's elegant 'probing' will be exemplary and his distinctive music will communicate unendingly as this echoic rhyming couplet sings:

> If I had to choose a bird call for reminding you,
> The greenshank's estuarial fluting would do.

Another poem, 'The New Window', has the poet looking out to his point of exit from this life:

> Sitting up in bed with binoculars I scan
> My final resting place in Dooaghtry
> Through the new window, soul-space

For my promontory, high and dry, Fairy
Fort the children called it, rising above
Otter-rumours and, now, the swan's nest
Among yellow flags, a blur of bog cotton,
Afterfeathers from a thousand preenings.

As a self-elegy it is a far cry from the triumphant, commanding style of
Yeats's self-regarding 'Under Ben Bulben'. Although the subject deals
with the poet's 'final' resting place in death, there is an energy and uplift
in the poem that speaks of vigorous life; as the poet's panoptic view
'scans' (from the Latin 'to climb') the hilly landscape, the movement of
the lines is perfectly paced in its own free-verse scansion; one supple
phrase flows in to the next, as the single sentence thrusts outwards and
upwards, soaring over the enjambment and so gesturing towards
something regenerative and free. The view from this 'new window' is
expansive and transformative; the common bog cotton of the field
wondrously appears to the fresh-eyed viewer as a drift of confetti-like
swans' feathers, while the promontory has been transfigured into a 'Fairy
Fort' in the imaginations of his children. A strong sense of the spiritual,
of the other-worldly, infuses Longley's recent poetry, and the form of
this hymn to life in the shadow of death liberates and releases the words
into the realm of the eternal.

'Altarpiece', published in the journal *The American Scholar*, fuses the
divine with the earthly, the realm of high art with the reality of war and
depredation. Here, the speaker stands in what must be the Basilica di
Santa Maria Gloriosa dei Frari in Venice viewing Titian's altarpiece of the
Madonna di Ca' Pesaro. The dazzling artistry of the painting's formal
design is such that the speaker (as viewer) becomes drawn into the
'diagonal drama' of this most dynamic of Renaissance artworks through
the gaze of a page-boy on the right-hand side who appears to be looking
out of it. However, there is more than this to catch the eye. The viewer
confesses to being 'distracted already' and has been hauled away from
the absorbing drama of Titian's artwork by the unsettling presence of a
bomb attached to the wall nearby; a shell dropped during World War I
that 'failed to explode'. The deeply unsettling proximity of art and atroci-
ty, beauty and horror, is driven home; the fact that even in this sacred
space, this haven of religion and art, the chaos of war and human hatred
will intrude and threaten to desecrate it:

The page-boy catches my eye before I go.
Buskers are serenading Mother and Child.
We need more angels, cloud-treaders, cherubic
Instrumentalists, bomb-disposal experts.
The sky is a minefield. We shall all get hurt.

Anything can come out of the sky, whether benign angel (as in the painting) or man-made explosive. But the truth of these inimical realities is there in the painting itself as it depicts the soldier being received by the saints; the Madonna and her saints are recognising Pesaro's achievement as commander of the papal fleet returned from a successful military campaign in the Venetian-Turkish war. The viewer of the painting is made to enter into the intractable truth of human existence: 'We shall all get hurt.' All that the artist can do is create and reveal the beauty and order around him and warn against its destruction.

For Longley, love is not merely a theme; it is integral to his poetic technique. For, what constitutes love but the ability to be attentive, the impulse to celebrate, to commemorate, to question and engage oneself fully, to study, to learn 'by heart', to reconcile and encourage peace, to warn and to protect, to devote oneself to others and extend oneself outwards? Longley's art is the art of love. Indeed, the relation between poetry and love, poetry and sex, has been central to his artistic vocation from its very beginning. Longley's poetic awakening as a teenager coincided with his sexual awakening; as he has recalled, he wrote his first bad poems as a sixteen-year-old to woo a girl he had fallen in love with. Poetry was – as it continues to be – born out of this impulse 'to explore experiences and feelings and share them with others'. Furthermore, poetry continues to be the 'sexy activity' – in his words – that it was when he first began writing. The act of bringing a poem into being is, for Longley, akin to the sexual act, a 'sensuous experience'. As he described the act of composition in an interview some years ago:

> I say the words aloud as I'm working with them. I roll them round in my mouth. [...] It's an erotic experience and I never know where it's going to take me. I don't know what shape the poem is going to be. I don't decide anything in advance. It's the most exciting thing in the world for me. In terms of pleasure it's more enjoyable than eating or drinking or sex even.

The thrill of love and of sexual longing is tangible in Longley's erotically-charged words. Longley is a poet who is in love with the things of the world and in love with language. As Wallace Stevens – who wrote many of his best poems in later life– wrote in *Adagia*: 'In poetry, you must love the words, the ideas and the images and rhythms with all your capacity to love anything at all'. Longley certainly does. As these newest poems demonstrate, Longley's delicate feeling for the movement of words is becoming more and more instinctive.

This is to be seen in a recently published elegy for Raymond Piper, 'Cloud Orchid'. The poem commemorates and celebrates their botanical friendship and grows out of four long stanzas of eleven lines, throughout which the enjambment stimulates surprise and vitality, while also, simultaneously, suggesting the broken articulation of the grief-struck mourner as it disrupts the verbal connections:

> Undistracted in your greenhouse-
> Studio by caterpillar
> Droppings from your mimosa tree
> That twisted overhead, you
> Gazed up through the branches and
> The broken pane imagining
> Your last flower portrait – 'for flowers
> Are good both for the living
> And the dead' – the miniscule
> Cloud Orchid that grows in the rain
> Forest's misty canopy.

Lines from Christopher Smart's buoyant 'Jubilate Agno' – set gloriously to music by a similarly inspired Benjamin Britten in his *Rejoice in the Lamb* cantata – sound throughout as heightened moments of lyricism that bind this friendship together in its own unique harmony of botanical terminology: 'ours was a language of flowers'. Longley brings Piper to life in this truly organic poem that unfolds itself through an unending reel of vignettes all depicting the magic and intimacy of their life together as explorers and discoverers. Yet there is a profound sadness here also, a sense that the death has come too soon, perhaps. This is further suggested by what to my ears are echoes of MacNeice's 'The Introduction' in the description of the 'caterpillar / droppings' from the 'tree / that twisted overhead'. MacNeice's frighteningly tactile lines are similarly contorted: 'Crawly crawly / went the twigs above their heads'. The last stanza of the poem comprises one long, multi-clausal question addressed to Piper cast in the intimate, conversational style that typifies the unselfconscious love between two friends. The poem ends hanging on a question mark, suspended, as, here again, the dead cannot answer back.

Two of Longley's most recent poems – 'A Hundred Doors' and 'Bee Orchid' – travel to Greece, to Paros and the 'Byzantine path'. This may be Longley sailing to Byzantium – his own 'search for the spiritual life' as Yeats put it – but, as before, he does so in a style that is quite different from that of his predecessor. Indeed, Longley may be seen to be updating some of Yeats's later key poems in his own poems of old age. In 'Bee Orchid', a contrast is set up in the opening lines between the hard stone of the 'marble pavement' and the vibrant plant and animal life that is flourishing all over it; 'camomile-strewn' as it is. Rather than concern himself with the art of that Byzantine civilisation as Yeats did, 'Bee

Orchid' has the poet and his companion on their knees in the dust on the Byzantine path as they try to locate, or 'look again' for, the elusive and ingenious flower of the title – the orchid is so-called because, as it evolved, it developed cunning contrivances to attract bees:

> Pollineum like a brain, the brainy
> Bumble-bee disguise. On our knees
> Among wild garlic, almost at prayer,
> We forgot about adder and lizard,
>
> And nearly missed in a juniper
> The blackcap's jet black. We waited
> And waited for his connoisseur's
> Restrained aria among the prickles.

The reader feels the same prolonged thrill of expectation – 'we waited / and waited' – as the lines of the poem breed themselves and move almost riotously over the breaks in order to detail the crazy, fecund natural life that lies before the orchid-seekers and is almost too plentiful for them to take in. The bee orchid eludes them to the end but the patient and alert are rewarded instead with the surprise appearance of a blackcap, and so they wait, in a not very comfortable auditorium ('among the prickles') in the hope of catching a live performance of this warbler's famed fluting music. The considerate devotion that Longley shows to all of the wondrous life of this earth, to the living and the dead, the minute and the immense, with such loving and studied detail, is returned to him by those who read his work with the same attentiveness and appreciative care. In the beautiful love poem to his second grandson, 'Christmas Tree', Longley tells the child: 'I put on specs to read your face'. Thus, to read, to study, to contemplate, is to love. As one reads Longley's latest work and considers his career to date, one is reminded of George Herbert's 'The Flower' – a poem described by Longley in his 2008 lecture 'A Jovial Hullabaloo' as 'one of the loveliest poems in the language': 'And now in age I bud again / After so many deaths I live and write.' This seems to me to encapsulate Longley's art as he enters old age; he continues to 'bud' and revitalise his art through love. As these latest poems show, Longley's love poems are not highly-stylised love letters. In their lively, instinctively musical style, they are akin to the complex mating-calls of birds; they are carefully-arranged love-posies, or, as he has described his elegies, 'wreaths'. His poems are as organic, as intricate and as ingenious as the bird calls and flowers that proliferate across his pages. 'I live hoping that there'll be another poem,' Longley has professed. One senses, as one delights in his most recent flowerings, that his finest poems are ahead of him.

Rosie Shepperd

THE LIMIT OF PERPETUAL SNOW
Nevis, West Indies

Morning comes on with three or four boys in the kitchen.
They've been here a while, talking high, gentle, throwing
thin soursop slices one to the other, their sweet hands
stretched out, laughing as the yellow fruit slips and drops
to the grey teak floor. The cook barks and his eyes roll.
'Pull them shutters. Is the syrup on the tables? Juice, boy?'

'Too early for the butter, Clovis, do you see the sun, boy?'
This is the best time; the smells and sounds of the kitchen.
Coconut trees creak and fan out from the night, hot rolls
rest while the shift girls gather toast cuts in baskets, throw
gold crusts to bananaquits. They love the sugar, never drop
one piece when they fly up like blue and yellow hands.

Cook wipes his face with the back and front of his hands.
One foot on a green corn can, he smiles in the shade as a boy
comes out of the cool room, carries thick white bowls of drop
scones and dishes of cut fruit. The girls reach into the kitchen,
hold doors for each other with one foot, white cloths thrown
over their shoulders. Violet lays out rows of sweet Danish rolls

and together we take in the ocean, take in the impossible rolls
of white horses on blue, the slowness of beach weed, my hand
as I lean from the pontoon to gather smooth stones and throw
one then another. Violet smiles, heads for the heat, the boys,
their games, the girls, their laughter, the cook and the kitchen.
She knows I'll stay here, skim stones in the sun. One, drop.

One, two, three, drop. Inside the reef, a pale blue boat drops
anchor, the crew spreads out, reels in sails. A girl swims, rolls
with the keel, then hangs on the ropes and calls to the kitchen.
One by one the boys come out, holding juice jugs in one hand.
They crinkle their eyes and laugh in the wind. The young boys
who came here from Spain? They loved the way the clouds threw

white on the mountain, like snow. They tried to climb up, throw
perpetual snow into the heat of the island, where the red drops
of Flamboyant cover crumbling walls of old plantations. The boys
gathered bunches of blossoms, wrapped with hibiscus and rolls
of palm leaf. These small flower parcels became gifts, handed
to friends like chicken with beans and rice from the kitchen.

I loved the throwaway chatter, the sounds of the kitchen, the boys
and their games; loved the girls and the smell of sweet raisin rolls,
dropped warm into baskets, loved the feel of the wind in my hand.

Rosie Shepperd

NIGHT FISHING

I have a friend who cries at night,
      says all kinds of things,
           like the next time her husband goes night fishing
                she'll lock him out.
         I want to tell her that she will be shut in,
                    only her face gets sort of shut up too,
                        jammed and so far past crying
like the door to the beach house that swelled up that winter.

You remember, don't you?
        How we couldn't get it open till we eased out the hinges,
           how rusted they were,
gummed up with crystals of
                salt and flaked steel.

One of the bolts had shorn right off but for the life of me,
           I couldn't see where it had fallen.
Perhaps, and I want to think this, it rolled away
        through the threads of your mother's rag rug,
           slipped down through the maple boards
               among hot water pipes,
                   a tangle of line, a salmon fly
                      hooked round a sand dollar,
        the skeleton of a sea-horse.

Daniel Hardisty

BURN AFTER READING

In the current sentence the words *current*,
sentence and *words* should be stressed,

at best a neutral emotional voice should
be used, simmering between bathwater

and day-old coffee. Diction should be precise,
avoiding regional variation, imagine

Lillie Langtry excusing herself to the W.C.
Picture the poem as a river that widens

dramatically as it reaches its Sound.
So you, too, must turn up the emotional heat

as you flow out to sea; highlighting,
as you go, any particularly fine images

that might escape the back row:
gulls held back by a hand of air, the sun as soap

washing away in the estuary's bowl.
Your goal is to raise saliva in the lip-wells

of the female attendees, at the very least
tears from the young or unmedicated.

Here tread the fine line, avoid the off beat,
outstare the cough that draws the listener off,

and should you find yourself alone,
seated, to no applause; six legs on the floor,

do not be defeated, sponged with gloom.
Pitch your voice lightly as

a balloon blown across the stage.
That last one really only works on the page.

George McWhirter

TURNIP HEAD

When do I keep turnips now in the fridge or root house
I improvised under the front steps' one-sided concrete
pyramid? The turnip head with its puce six o'clock
shadow, fleshy brow and top knot, chunky chin
and tapered brain – a barbarian's, a visigoth's,
I decapitated and gouged out with a potato peeler
when I was a spalpeen.

I dug into the crown with a cheap dagger,
then circled the peeler round the hole I made
till there was only an inch of its rind-skull left
for me to knife in the eyes, nose,
then hilt in hand, pause
for the slice at a mouth and to consider
how many teeth to put in.

> Kin ye see, now, turniphead?
> Then, scare whoever the hell
> ye see off our stoop.

Cut and mashed I ate it, like a grousing cannibal
whose kill had gone off, the blood dulled
to an off-golden podge, winking at me
off too many dinner plates – as if it held
left-over ideas
from the head it came from.

Fed-up and afraid of committing
turnip turpitude I fled to the land
of the grand bland pumpkin,
but with hard mouth, teeth and stabbing tongue,
many an evening I have turned my talk
into a heavy, carved-up turnip
in order to send something frightening
out the door, a lumpy memento

of my vision, to scare those who perceive it
on the stoop, if they ever return to the lit-up eyes,
the stench of burning turnip on my lips

and me sitting, fleshy brow and ginger jaw,
product of a bitter clime,
a poor man's pumpkin.

Susan Donnelly

THE SIDE ALTARS

St Joseph, at the left,
holds the miraculous
flowering staff
that showed him chosen

for Mary, who stands
on Earth's globe,
blue-robed, at the right.

She, whom I badgered
throughout adolescence
with please-make-him-call,

looks heavenward,
the serpent under her feet.

Before each statue,
candles in red shot glasses.
Clink of a nickel
into the tin box,
lighters in sand,

wish candle
begun from another
already burning.

Did I say 'wish'?
Prayer.

Susan Donnelly

THE BEGGING GIRL

The whole time I've sat here
at the coffee shop window
no one's given her anything.
It puts people off, that jivey,
almost-dance as she comes up,
with a smile that says you and she
share a joke. In her twenties
probably, good clothes, fresh-faced,
            but awry somehow,
like the way she spoke
just now, as I came from the bank
any sweeties? something like that
I didn't quite catch, and startled,
– do I know her? –
I hurried past, since it was pouring.
Most people don't even stop,
Only one starts to talk with her,
then, step by step, backs away.
Whenever the sidewalk's empty,
she stops jigging, walks under rain
in a slow circle. Her head is bent.
She doesn't pull up her hood.

Ralph Black

from AUTOMOTIVE HAIKU

1.
Just east of Hartford,
Stevens's 14th blackbird
Clucks at the traffic.

2.
As for the scooter
Careening for the centre:
Vespas splaticus.

3.
Damn it all, Dublin!
Let Molly coddle your cars.
Quit these quaint cobbles.

4.
Oh, my Romeo.
My jade Alfa Romeo.
Grind my 2nd gear.

5.
At dawn, nightingales
Rev their delicate engines:
Liquid ellipses.

6.
Six cuckoos nesting
In the circled shrubbery:
Six cars stalled at noon.

7.
East of the city:
Monks rake gravel into swirls
Resembling roads.

8.
Traffic got you down?
Li Po, punting up the Thames,
Finds a smoother way.

9.
Tonight the full moon
Will ignite every windshield
On the Champs-Élysées.

10.
Last month in Brussels
Jack Kerouac was spotted
Hitching counter-clockwise.

11.
When the chicken truck
Crashed, the chickens kept walking –
Tarred beaks to the tarmac.

12.
Certain roundabouts
Bloom with weeds, cinders, and ash:
Others bare as grief.

13.
The Fiat's tiny wheels,
Like hockey pucks skirling
The black iced-rinked road.

14.
A late summer rain
Brings out the frogs, hiccupping
Into the headlights.

15.
In the blue-inked sea
Cephalopodian roads
Waver like eel grass.

16.
Sartre coasts into
A Parisian roundabout –
All his *sorties* X-ed.

17.
One wonders which cars
Once circled Stonehenge, and how
Their lithic wheels rolled.

18.
The shepherd's herded
Herd went weird waiting for word
From the shearing shed.

19.
At the traffic light,
A Hummer and Mini rev:
A bison and a bee.

Paul Grattan

A DEVIL'S PURSE
  – for Maire Frances

*In 1629 Valentine Payne wrote the Earl of Kildare that he had built a Quay at
Strangford, 'where there was none before. The biggest shippe that the King hathe,
may lay her side beside it.'*

i. Cuan

It was an Ards Peninsula town –
the strong fiord some Viking named
after a season's rapine, stars
countable, attuned to the huffings
of a kelp-quilted lough, a Cheyne-
Stokes breathing for lost Londonderrys
and Castlewards, the last December
of ourselves alone.

ii. Walter's rock

UP DOWN the rock sings, out past Killyleagh,
past plumes of smoke an abused chip-pan painted
sky-high
              aye but they were home-made chips boy
and by the water where we wheel our first and only daughter
swaddled up rightly in her granny's coy, clotted Ulster-
Scots, my heid loups in an accent muted by this bay
              thrawn as a box of crabs.

iii. The Portaferry Stane

Babs will tell you, Babs who has brought Dalmatians,
tomato and scrumpy chutney, with auld decency will tell you
polluted by drink on Stephen's Day we are not. We have taken
the ecstasy of jingle bells on bird-black beaches to the point
where arguments whip atomies of soot into the Jacobean keep
of the Demesne. And the bonny moorhen is hooked, half-minded
to quit the Narrows definitely this year, this sack-clothed January.
While a boy from the Markets bobs and is lost to his Da', waist-
deep in briny grief and the keening of Mass Cards, who is to say
will not bring comfort, cold or cod, to a coffin's bass relief.

iv. The Corner Boy's Gift for Bifurcation

On Windmill Hill three craws survey a road still ca'd a brae
in Greba, until the world is filled with cawing thaumaturgy. Christ
if ever I said I could murder a crow, forgive me. Mind, yon time
in Carrowdore we parked our Southern plate under their arch
to ask directions for the Kirk. Lively we counted coppers
for ten Purple, not to speak of the Fat Frog, while Louis moldered
in his grave and hard men with mullets, *aye ready*, took their bevy
outside, misreading Kildare for Kerry, keeping the Kingdom true.

v. Afore ye go

We shot the craw, loving the crush of noses against windshield.
At Ardkeen you folded white roses in childhood pockets, pinching
the cold mantle's cheek for old times sake. The Cur passed us
on the Ballybeen Express, a belly on him like a poisoned pup, eyes
peeled shut, doing seventy in a bone-shook Ulsterbus. Poets
are liars right enough, but what would the Queen make of the Irish
at the beginning or gable end of the Estate, *lámh dearg abú*
the stone throwers fate unbreakable, moving a schoolgirl to tears.

vi. Eurydice

Darby and Joan, in the bleached formica
of their new kitchen. Six bells, eye water spilt
upon the table. She is gone daft watching
her weans pitch and toss beyond the versed out
town, first Liverpool then Dublin. *Fender Park'll*
dae me love is how the all clear sounds fae Scrabo
Tower tae Cowey's Wells, *as green grows the grass*
                                below the gantries oh.

vii. Orpheus

Blair Mayne was a hula-maiden for a Magus so,
his long range desert sass cast in grass-skirted, pelvic-
thrust for the Millennium. *We give artists grants to imagine*
war heroes in leafy bowers, the Jolly Judge explodes. Fu'
Orpheus chaps, has taken his punishment for house-
breaking, can be forgiven but not forgotten for turning
his back on her long fair hair, on My Lady's Road,
chucking a theory of strings for the patter of Powers.

viii. Clough

Small towns have long memories jegs in your craw, rattles
past Clough and something Pop says doesn't bare thinking.
A body in a stour, standing closer than a father should
in the school returning gloom, stoops to hood some wee lad.
Inequities of pottery, wild celery, motte and bailey, a slue
of tin-white cement sacks, old enough to be grist, now laid
to rest with the best mutant Ards statistics. *Living here*
you'd kill me, you protest, putting your foot down, *pack it in.*

ix. The Decommissioning of the Boats

Committed to mud and memory, we've had our fill
of holly on the Mastheads. *Transcend, Laharoi, Advantage,*
yon auld licht lighted up like a pagan Longship. War
whole, shivering timbers tarred with the same brush
that beached the *Corner Boy*, burnt prows and bulldozed
sprits fae Ardglass, Portavogie; black-coated workers,
game's a bogie. For decommissioned berth, take this touch-
tank; nursehound, skate, ray, play empty pursed beside us.

Diane Fahey

AT THE CLIFFS

I'd hoped for a marsh harrier, keeping
its place in the wind – a bookmark between
airy pages – or some voyager from
Antarctica, in its white glide the carved
silence of ice. My gaze hovers, swoops
over that crack in the sea: a faultline
of foam, jagged as a gull's flight through storm.

The rip tracks shorewards, past where surfers
skate and bounce along glass arcades,
skidding down as snowy paws clamber
towards the rock-shelf – beyond which the dunes,
fragile haunt of the red-cap, ascend through
marram reefs to these cliffs: laced with gale-blown
shell grit; algae; the bones of fish and birds.

Anamaría Crowe Serrano

MY OPIA

in the diagram
the red line A ends abruptly
between
vision and the sky
                poised
on a transversal plane
trans-genred verse
where understanding should be
located

if it is a measurement of sight
my eye has been reduced
to its curvature
        points in a socket
and I flounder, blindly

following little arrows that point
to links
between the membrane, K
and distance, a radial row
of decimals that are
supposedly
        pieces of pie

mathematical truths crumble
off the edge of my formulae
leaving me

curious
        not about the line
but the space that surrounds it
the unpartnered parenthesis
hurling its contents
into emptiness

Anamaría Crowe Serrano

i.m. ANNE LEAHY

it can happen any day
that you drop in
larger than life, beaming
the silence vociferously past me

but I have no stops to pull
that might change a thing
not a one
– my fingers are numb –
just a hunger for the freshness
of your skin
the lustre of your hair
a sentence half-begun
stuck in the broken circuitry
of a life that fell
just short
of opportunity

the organ booms cankerous
round the vaults
and you play it wild, sublime
but secular enough
to keep the regulars lingering
recognising passion as it strains
to break free of body
bricks and mortar

here's a word I don't understand: lung
breathing big like Sundays
loud, the voice pushing
through the trachea

and something else
I don't understand: the sound
of morning when word came

the acoustics of that finality
butchering the day

Rebecca O'Connor

THE LAKES

The wet here can break a person's heart with sheer persistence.
Imagine one day your husband's beard smells of damp dog,
his long johns stink of pondweed, and you think nothing –
or very little – of it. Until, one day,
you wake to find him looking up at you with wet spaniel eyes.
That's what it's like – an endless incoming tide.
The trick is to give him plenty of exercise.

Fergus Allen

SANCREED

Some resolution is needed to get there
along the foot-wide track, past stinging nettles,
bracken and garlic mustard, over stiles,
under elder infected with Jew's-ear,
to reach the pool where Balin le Savage
could not water his exhausted gelding,
the treacherous stone steps down to the well
being slippery as the smile of Morgan le Fay.
He fetched up his helmet, filled to the brim,
but the parched brute could only wet its tongue
and stand and puff and steam among the brambles.

Now it's known as the wishing well, where locals
tie hankies, neckties, eggshells, coloured rags
and necklets of plastic beads to the twigs
of the overhanging crab-tree – but magical
all the same, its antennae tuned to yearning.
The girls giggle as they attach their tokens,
though deep inside they stretch imagined hands
into the mists where the future is formed,
hoping the rules will bend to their desires.
But the years ahead of them already know
just where the crow's feet are going to walk.

Neil Curry

from SOME LETTERS NEVER SENT

To: Timothy the Tortoise, 'The Wakes', Selborne, Hampshire

No end of letters came for Mr White,
Which is why this one, Timothy, is aimed
At you, somewhere, I hope, in his garden,
Under the broad beans perhaps, or if you're
Really lucky and nobody's noticed as yet,
Happily chomping away among the strawberry beds.

He'd grown very fond of you, you know,
And as autumn came and the days darkened,
He'd watch out for where you went burrowing
Down into the warmth of the compost heap,
Safely stowing your legs in under your own self's roof,
Ready for what he unkindly called your 'joyless stupor'.

Joyless? I wonder what he thought you would
Be missing out on: chilblains, chapped hands, ice
And snow? Mr W himself woke
One morning to find the water frozen
Solid in his bedside decanter. When spring came though
He'd be eager to greet you, announcing in his Journal:

'Timothy did come forth and march about.'
Hibernation was a constant puzzle
To him. Swallows? Africa? Surely not.
At times you caught the rougher end of this
Spirit of enquiry. Being dunked into a pail
Of water to see if you could swim must have been nasty.

But for the most part, Timothy, you had
An easy life. No one harnessed you up
To pull a plough, or ever expected
You to bark, grow wool, lay eggs, or catch mice.
And as for your master – even at the risk of death
From cholera, typhoid, smallpox, or mumps, I would

Gladly swap lives with him; take on his worries:
Was it *true* that bats would fly down people's
Chimneys to gnaw at the bacon hanging
In their kitchens? Naturalist-cum-parson-
cum-poet, yes, I think I could manage that. I'd preach
The Wisdom of God as Manifest in His Creation.

Consider the divine economy
shown in that most lowly of amphibians
the frog: aquatic first, it sinuates
the tail of a fish; but, when his legs appear,
that same appendage, deemed useless now, drops off
and the creature doth betake itself to land. Sorry, I

Got carried away a bit then. Before
You toddle off though to snooze in the forests
Of asparagus, let me echo Gilbert's
Closing words to his friend Mr Pennant
And assure you that every incident
Which occasions a renewal of our correspondence
Will ever be pleasing and agreeable to me.

Tom French

RUSTY FITZPATRICK
  – to Max O'Connell, Shep Hanrahan, Zebedee McGurk and Cocoa O'Briain

  'Today, many adult film stars maintain that fluffers are a thing of the past,
  needed in the 1970s and 1980s when the crew, shooting on celluloid, needed
  much more time to prepare a shot.' – Wikipedia

The lives we can barely begin to imagine begin
with our first pets' names and our mothers' maiden
ones, and spiral from there to the money shot
with a handycam, and realistic lighting in

en suites with hourly rates on outskirts and verges
of hamlets we can claim to have never been in
because we came and went in tinted *4x4s*
with entourages of body doubles and fluffers

outside of daylight hours, and go on until
they end with the next crop of up-and-comers
praising our stamina, soliciting autographs

we fire off as though the names we wrote were
not the Christian names we gave our animals
nor the names our mothers answered to as girls.

Tom French

EXPRESS

I could have no more told your new house from the train
across the wheat fields changing to gold from green
than I could the line of the horizon from the line of the rails
nor told, with any degree of certainty, where the train
in question may have been going, from whence it came.
All I'd seen was one engine hauling another backways
through the wheat fields changing from gold to green.

Zoë Landale

BUTE INLET

The river says: water parts air the way old flesh slides
from bones. Coincides. High up the bank you bend
to an extended line of flotsam, what are these grey arrows

the size and texture of a narrow boot toe?
You flinch when you see back-facing serrations. Teeth.
Then you know: salmon noses transformed to rubber,

embers of the eyes long gone, cheek plates
giant scales. Ankle deep, these are the lavish dead.
You pick one up, translate detail as well your

own internal shift between *before*, seeing the heads'
shapes as abstraction and beautiful, and the flinch.
Being led to see closely is a form of loving.

Seasons mean a live ring rotates between inlet and icefield.
Winters, the river rearranges the valley floor
with the peeled delicacy of the inevitable, say a dam

buckling, the trickle turning to a slam of water,
utter disintegration, only here is just riprap and roads,
the wisdom of gravel bars which forgive alterations

though they don't forget aberration,the river's
variableness and turning. Yearning to see grizzlies amble
onto gravel bars and scoop out slivers of light; salmon.

August penstemmon bloom. Within the ring, fireweed and thistle
seeds ascend in linked white clusters, buoyant as prayers,
an epistle to the glaciers; the days exceed yearning.

Bob Dylan

ÁILTEOIR / JOKERMAN

'Seasamh ar an uisce ag teilgean aráin
Is na súile i gcloigeann iarainn an íoláin ag spréachadh
Báid chian' ag gabháil isteach sa cheo
Saolaíodh tú le nathair id' dhá dhóid
Agus hairicín ag séideadh
Níl an tsaoirse ach coiscéim coilligh uait
Ach leis an bhfírinne ar iarraidh cad is fiú í a lua.

Rinc a Áilteoir le ceol an fhiliméala
Eitilse a éin faoi sholas na ré,
ó, ó, ó a Áilteoir.

Nach mear mar a ghabhann an ghrian fé sa spéir
Éiríonn tú suas 's ní deir slán féin le héinne.
Mar ná leagfadh aingil cos gabhann baotháin
A dtodhchaí araon chomh lán scátha, rud nach léir ort.
Sraith amháin eile craicinn á chur agat
Ag coimeád chun tosaigh ar an ngéarleantóir atá ionat.

Rinc a Áilteoir le ceol an fhiliméala
Eitilse a éin faoi sholas na ré,
ó, ó, ó a Áilteoir.

Is fear tú ón sliabh, a shiúlaíonn ar na néalta,
Ionramhálaí céadta, camann tú brionglóidí
Taoi ag triall ar Sodom is Gomorrah
Ach is cuma leat, níl éinne ann arb fhonn leis
do dheirfiúr a phósadh
Cara mairtírigh, cara le bean na haithise
Féachann tú isteach sa bhfoirnéis laomtha, chíonn an fear saibhir
   gan aon ainm.

Rinc a Áilteoir le ceol an fhiliméala
Eitilse a éin faoi sholas na ré,
ó, ó, ó a Áilteoir.

Bhuel Leabhar úd Léivític agus Deotranaimí
Dlí an dufair agus an dlí muirí amháin a mhúinfidh tú
I ndeatach an idirsholais ar each lachtbhán
Michelangelo amháin a dhéanfadh d'éadan a dhealbhú
Ag glacadh scíth sna goirt, i bhfad ón láthair shuaite,
Leath id shuan faoi na réalta is cú beag ag lí do ghrua-sa

Rinc a Áilteoir le ceol an fhiliméala
Eitilse a éin faoi sholas na ré,
ó, ó, ó a Áilteoir.

Tá an fear raidhfil sa tóir ar bhacach is easlán
Mar atá an préitseálaí, ní léir cé a bheidh sa chéad áit,
Bataí oíche is canónacha uisce, deoirghás, ceapghlas
Manglaim Molotov agus carraigeacha laistiar de gach dallán,
Breithiúna bréige 'fáil bháis sna lusnaí a shníomhaid
Níl ann ach seal 'dtí go siúlaíonn isteach an oích'.

Rinc a Áilteoir le ceol an fhiliméala
Eitilse a éin faoi sholas na ré,
ó, ó, ó a Áilteoir.

Tá an domhan seo lán scáthanna, na spéartha slim liath,
Do bhean inniu saolaíodh triath, is i ndearg a ghléas sí é.
Cuirfidh sé an sagart ina phóc', is an lann leis an dtine
Bainfidh sé den tsráid na leanaí gan bhuime
Is fágfaidh iad ag cosa meirdrí.
Ó a Áilteoir tuigeann tú cad tá aige á lorg
Ó a Áilteoir ní thugann tú aon tor' air.

Rinc a Áilteoir le ceol an fhiliméala
Eitilse a éin faoi sholas na ré,
ó, ó, ó a Áilteoir.

– translation by **Colm Breathnach** of Bob Dylan's 'Jokerman'

Bob Dylan

BHEITH ISTIGH ÓN STOIRM / SHELTER FROM THE STORM

Saol eile ar fad a bhí ann, sclábhaíocht agus cró
Suáilce ab ea an dorchacht
Is bhí guta ar an ród.
Isteach liom ón bhfiántas
Mar neach a bhí gan fhoirm:
Gabh i leith, ar sí, is tabharfad duit
Bheith istigh ón stoirm.

Má chastar orm aris í
M'fhocal duit 's mo lámh
Go ndéanfadsa mo dhícheall di
Oíche agus lá.
I ndomhan na súl crua marbh
Bíonn teas ar fáil sa choirm:
Gabh i leith, ar sí, is tabharfad duit
Bheith istigh ón stoirm.

Ní raibh húm ná hám eadrainn
Ná ceachtar againn i mbaol
Ná freagra agam ar aon ní
'Bhí ag tarlú i mo shaol;
Samhlaigh anois duit féinig
Áit teolaí agus tirim:
Gabh i leith, ar sí, is tabharfad duit
Bheith istigh ón stoirm.

Bhíos tuirseach traochta tnáite
Flichshneachta i mo ghruaig
Bhíos im líbín báite
Chuir siad orm an ruaig.
Bhíos creachta i mo chrogall dom
Mar Pholl na Bró i mBoirinn
Gabh i leith, ar sí, is tabharfad duit
Bheith istigh ón stoirm.

Sea chasas i mo thimpeall
Is b'iúd í romham sa tslí
Bráisléad ar chaol a láimhe
B'í plúr na mban donn í.
Bhain an ainnir shéimh ansin díom
An choróin spíne a bhí orm:
Gabh i leith, ar sí, is tabharfad duit
Bheith istigh ón stoirm.

Tá falla éigin eadrainn
Rud nach léir ar lár.
Dheineas gamal ceart díom féinig
Is cóir dom é a rá
Smaoinigh siar, a gharsúinín,
Smaoinigh, cé nach n-oireann:
Gabh i leith, ar sí, is tabharfad duit
Bheith istigh ón stoirm.

Bheul, luíonn an bhróg ar an ionadaí
Is an praeitseálaí ar a each
Ach níl bun ná barr le haon ní
Ach le Lá an Luain, mo chreach.
Tá an t-adhlacóir ar leathshúil
Ach cleachtann sé a ghairm:
Gabh i leith, ar sí, is tabharfad duit
Bheith istigh ón stoirm.

Is do chuala mé báibíní
Is iad ag caoineadh leo
Is na seandaoine dóite
Is iad ar strae sa cheo
An dtuigimse do chás, a chroí,
Bhfuil deireadh anois le hurraim?
Gabh i leith, ar sí, is tabharfad duit
Bheith istigh ón stoirm.

Is i mBaile an Bhuinnéanaigh
Gan bhalcaisí gan phóg
Mo shlánú a bhí uaimse
Is fuaireas ródháileog
Do bhíos i m'uainín íobartha
Is díoladh mé le scorn:
Gabh i leith, ar sí, is tabharfad duit
Bheith istigh ón stoirm.

Bhuel, táim i bhfad ó bhaile anois
Ach tá teorainn os mo chomhair
Ar chonair chaol na hÁilleachta
Is mé ag dul thar fóir.
Dá mbeadh breith agam ar m'aiféala
Ní bheinn anseo go doirbh:
Gabh i leith, ar sí, is tabharfad duit
Bheith istigh ón stoirm.

– translation by **Gabriel Rosenstock** of Bob Dylan's 'Shelter from the Storm'

IMRAM Féile Litríochta Gaeilge a choimisiúnaigh na haistriúcháin seo le Gabriel Rosenstock agus Colm Breathnach ar amhráin de chuid Bhob Dylan. Ba iad Liam Ó Maonlaí agus Caoimhín Mac Giolla Catháin a chan ar dtús iad sa Crawdaddy, BÁC, Dé Domhnaigh, 27 Meán Fómhair 2009. Steve Cooney a bhí i mbun cóirithe.

These translations of Dylan songs by Gabriel Rosenstock and Colm Breathnach were commissioned by the **IMRAM Irish Language Literature Festival.** They were first performed by singers Liam Ó Maonlaí and Caoimhín Mac Giolla Catháin to arrangements by Steve Cooney on Sunday 27 September 2009 at Crawdaddy in Dublin.

Bill Tinley

WHAT IS MEANT BY HOME

Derek Mahon, *Life on Earth* (Gallery Books, 2008), €11.95.

In 'Homage to Goa', the closing poem in Derek Mahon's new collection, *Life on Earth*, the poet characterises his younger self as 'a cheeky monkey keen on human thought' who would 'dance / wildly at times'. To those familiar with Mahon's work this is a reminder of the poet who blazed with verbal and intellectual intensity in his early collections, notably *Lives* and *The Snow Party*. More than three decades on and a somewhat avuncular Mahon looks back on that angrier, younger man and sees a 'mozzie' who 'buzzed and bit'. It's an affectionate putting of himself in place rather than a dismissal of his youthful self.

Mature Mahon squirts insect repellent at mosquitoes as he takes his ease in Goa under a cooling fan or 'rock[s] on a warm veranda as daylight goes.' The caustic poet of 'Rage for Order' and 'The Apotheosis of Tins' has mellowed to one transfixed by ripening fruit, cloud movements and solar power. 'An ageing man repents his wicked ways' he tells us, via Abu al-Ma'ari, excusing perhaps the drop in voltage in Mahon's poetry since a long silence was broken in 1995 with the publication of *The Hudson Letter*. In place of a poetry crackling with linguistic energy and a current of dystopian rage we have now a more contemplative perspective on the world and the people who inhabit it. At a formal level there is not much surprise in this. *The Hunt by Night*, published in 1982, was already a transformation from the guiding principles of Mahon's 1970s collections. A poem of such unique brilliance as 'Ovid in Tomis' looked and read all the more distinctive in the company of work increasingly tuned to a Lowellian register. 'Courtyards in Delft', 'A Garage in Co Cork' and 'The Globe in North Carolina' negotiated a territory between measured public utterance and private expression of social and political disenchantment.

Mahon's prosodic gifts sustained the discursive sequences of the 1990s, a Swiftian engagement with *fin-de-siècle* life in New York and Dublin not quite concealing the essential superficiality of such verse. While *The Hudson Letter* and *The Yellow Book* were energised by a new lease of bohemian life, recalling at times the jauntiness of early poems from *Night-Crossing*, perhaps their most remarkable feature was the fact that Mahon surrounded himself with people: not the select coterie of artistic exemplars such as Camus and Munch but the anonymous masses, whether cooped up in apartments or homeless on the streets of the metropolis. Clearly, the abrasiveness of early Mahon has been tempered. He has moved in from the periphery and if he is still far from the centre there is nevertheless a more relaxed and patient aspect to his work. Clouds dominate *Harbour Lights* and they are much in evidence in *Life on Earth* as well. It is no coincidence that Mahon sees them and remarks on them so frequently. In the past he looked beyond them to the celestial wastes, searching for answers in the stars and usually finding no more than a rebuke to our cosmic insignificance. Now, however, the 'bowl of cloud' that represented oblivion for the forgotten mushrooms of a Co Wexford shed seems to captivate the poet. The distance between man and what he looks to for meaning has foreshortened dramatically. If Mahon relishes the shifting, intangible dreaminess of clouds – one is reminded at times of John Banville's superb descriptions of skyscapes in *Eclipse* – their primary relevance here is as a context for the poet's increasing concern for environmental issues.

Mahon's 'eco-poetry', as the blurb has it, addresses this topic most directly in the sequence 'Homage to Gaia'. Calling on the sun in the 'post-petroleum age' to 'Remember life on Earth!', the poet marvels at the potential to harness its 'radiant energies' for the benefit of man. But environmental positives can be offset by poetic flat-footedness:

> so even an average annual
> thousand kilowatt hours
>   per photovoltaic panel
>
> looks feasible in time.

That mouthful might be good news on the lips of a Green Party minister but as poetry it's biodegradable. Of far more consequence is the distinction in the second part of the sequence between people and planet: 'we babble about the world / while you sustain the earth.' 'Sand and Stars', the fourth section, exemplifies what motivates mature Mahon. Inclined to have an early night the poet is nevertheless tuned in to the 'cold strand, / the vast sky' outside. The man-made town, flickering in the darkness, loses its dimensions when seen from a different perspective:

> As for the twinkly town,
>
> roofed like a sea surface
>   with moonlit tiles, the eye
> measures its tiny houses
>   against an enormous sky.

Suddenly, Mahon has imagined Kinsale as a post-climate-change Atlantis where, mischievously, 'plaice flap in the ruins / of sunken bungalows.'

In 'At Ursula's', a small spanner is thrown into the eco-works. As 'Boats strain at sea, alas, / gales rattle the slates', Mahon is safe from the elements as he snugly contemplates 'some amusing fusion / Thai and Italian both'. Aren't 'local' and 'seasonal produce' the environmental buzz-words? This playfulness segues into a take on London deluged by a 'corporate and imported' rain where the poet, in an echo of 'The Mayo Tao', has

...checked for days

on the speaking, anachronistic
    fate of a paint blister
scraped and flaking into
    a heap of dust and plaster.

An eye for the minute detail recharges the sequence, its poetry in the lateral strands and tangents. Notwithstanding his bohemian credentials, Mahon occasionally comes across as a crusty old conservative so it is hugely surprising to find him writing in admiration of the Icelandic singer, Björk. In perhaps the finest poem in *Life on Earth*, 'Ode to Björk' casts her as 'Dark bird of ice, dark swan / of snow' whose ethereal voice dismisses the 'expectations / of corporate brainwash rock.' Björk's defiant individuality is a triumph for 'mystery and mystique, / the hidden places where / the wild things are'. Mahon presents her as an incarnation of Gaia, of Mother Earth, keening to the Arctic night:

Up there where silence falls
    and there is no more land
your scared, scary voice calls
    to the great waste beyond.

This is a brief convergence of Mahon's concerns about environmental change, his rejection of uniformity and corporate slavishness, and the stark imagery that made poems such as 'An Image from Beckett' and 'The Snow Party' so compelling.

The figure of the solitary female communicating to a 'beyond' is established in the first poem here, 'Ariadne on Naxos', another Mahon take on Ovid, in which the abandoned speaker wonders 'will some kind god take pity on me'. Gaia too, like Ariadne and Björk, may be at the limit of endurance, screaming into a waste in which there may be no one to hear or take heed. Only Mahon's renewed pleasure in the company of mankind and his preference for 'here' over the 'beyond' of paradise tempers this bleakness.

In 'A Country Road', one of the finer pieces in *Life on Earth*, Mahon considers the question of man's place on the planet. Is existence nothing more than a puzzle we must solve, a 'show ... set out for our grand synthesis'? Are we separate from or part of the earth? In early poems Mahon saw humans as nothing more than a temporary but destructive presence, intruders the non-human world looked upon with grim forbearance as it waited on our extinction. Now he asserts:

We belong to this –

not as discrete
observing presences but as born
participants in the action...

While 'Animal, vegetable, mineral watch / as we walk their patch', the detritus we have created is part of the process and nature's absorption of our rubbish – 'Abandoned trailers', 'a bath in the woods' – is neither rejection nor defeat but rather a sign that 'we belong here too'.

All that rubbish is, in one sense, what previous Mahon poems have left behind. Always one to revise his work his revisiting of familiar items becomes an entirely appropriate form of recycling. The dredged up material is reworked and contributes to a substantial re-adjustment of Mahon's poetic vision.

At times this re-handling of old material can seem unnecessary. In another sequence, 'Art Notes', Mahon revives 'A Lighthouse in Maine', first collected in *The Hunt by Night* but omitted from *Collected Poems*. The slender tercets of the original are remoulded into altogether more 'squat' pentameter octets, and while this may seem like a coincidence of form and theme, the effect is not beneficial. Notwithstanding his sense of Hopper's lighthouses as 'squat', their most obvious characteristics are surely their uprightness and relative leanness. Furthermore, the journey Mahon urges on the reader was better suggested by the rangy layout of lithe stanzas in the original version. But Mahon's dalliances with paintings are rarely without merit. Revisiting Magritte's *L'Empire des Lumières*, which adorned the cover of his Jaccottet translations, Mahon makes much of the simple act of just looking and patient exploration. Speaking as Nicolas de Staël, he brings us back to a familiar realm of inanimate objects finding, *a lá* Van Gogh, expression in the world of painting:

Here I renounce abstraction, turning again
to the world of objects, to the stoical souls
of candlesticks and jugs, bottles and bowls.

Various other re-writings and retrievals in *Life on Earth* are less engaging. In 'Brian Moore's Belfast' we might have hoped for some productive conjunction of personal recollections of the poet's home town and the work of a novelist much admired by Mahon but the poem is merely nostalgic. 'Biographia Literaria' inevitably invites comparison with 'De Quincey in Later Life' but the fluidity and edge of the early poem are not replicated in a piece hamstrung by the formal template Mahon applies to much of his post-1980s work. Yet there are signs he may be loosening his commitment to a shape he commands with such ease that it was bound to engender a certain staidness. And how much better might 'Quaderno' be without the shackles of rhymed pentameters? The lightness and directness suggested by a writer's notebook are swamped by formal uniformity.

Where the poetic charge is sufficiently urgent, as in 'Goa', Mahon's mastery of form finds its mark:

> Do you laze this evening on an 'azure' shore,
> you whom I last saw twenty years ago,
> or contemplate from a beach house in Goa
> the Indian Ocean breaking on the coast
> where my love, gratitude and grief lie waste?

The syntactical dexterity, the beautifully balanced lines – reminiscent of 'Achill' – deployed in the service of love and loss, remind us of Mahon at his best. And it shows too that when his attention is turned to individual human beings inhabiting this vulnerable planet there is a grandeur in Mahon's work that sets him apart. As he puts it in 'Research', disdaining the prospect of 'ice in the Sea of Rains', here 'on Earth / we've mud, plants, pleasure, pain / and even real lives to be getting on with'.

Siobhán Campbell

NO DANGER OF ELEGY

Mary O'Malley, *A Perfect V* (Carcanet, 2006), £8.95.
Moya Cannon, *Carrying the Songs* (Carcanet, 2007), £9.95.
Paula Meehan, *Painting Rain* (Carcanet, 2009), £9.95.

The idea of home and the dismantling of the notions surrounding it are crucial to the overall thrust of the poems in Mary O'Malley's *A Perfect V*, many of which are animated by a speaking voice that is, by turns, fiercely angry and coolly humorous.

'Home? There is no danger of elegy' ('On Friar's Hill') could be a coda for the collection where the poet appears to be playing with the real power of negative passion and its implications. Many of these pieces emerge from a pressurised moment, when 'Cunning / life has us outfoxed', a line that captures the syntactical oddity O'Malley sometimes employs to amplify her intent. This poem, entitled 'Separation', ends with a dark humour which becomes a characteristic move that this poet makes: 'Where is the photographer, the ludicrous cake?'

The protagonist, who we might presume is the poet herself, is almost unbearably aware of what is at stake. The key question may be: if we dismantle the illusion of meaning, what will be left? For an artist, this will always be related to the work itself: 'Who would unstitch a tune from its haunting?' ('The De Danann Tapestries'). In this way, a trajectory that may have once been a personal journey becomes a meditation on how the poem may serve the real experience of human pain.

Various answers are proffered. 'The News from Titan' supposes 'there is no interior' and asks, 'What if the Titans are flourishing…and those pictures they sent back / are just elaborate jokes?' In 'Birthday Poem 2003', the 'he', let down by words, has to dream himself 'back to a boat':

> …The ribs
> mark his belly and his hand curls
> around the rowel pin.

Another poet might have left the piece, pleased with the elegiac moment, but that will not be enough in *A Perfect V*, which insists on bringing the reader back to the intractable:

> We start again
> with the old instructions:

first build a boat. *No*, he says,
first catch your tree.

While the question, 'What is the place of art?' is palpable throughout, there is also great fun to be had. 'The Jack of Hearts' is spittingly bitter but saved by a knowing self-mockery and absolute control of the line. 'Communion at the Gate Theatre' is a piece which will surely be anthologised, as it places the protagonist at the one production of *Hamlet* which every Leaving Certificate student in Ireland is up from the country to attend. 'A generation of throwbacks…without Latin to sustain them', our heroine thinks, while trying to leave after calling out abuse to Hamlet, only to find, after checking the exits, that 'the half-formed faces' are devout, and that a moment of true communion can still happen through all the awfulness. It is those rare and earned moments that animate the most memorable lines in this collection. Unafraid to draw the reader close to the flame of real feeling, this poet knows too when to cool things down and rely on the music of the lyric or the emotional click as a well-turned phrase steadies a line. I will carry the 'promise of a fingerclip moon' with me from my reading of O'Malley, as well as the sense that this whole book is 'a wave / between dark and dark in this diamond of time.'

Moya Cannon's spare, meditative style is something which has made her an immediately recognisable voice since her earlier collections, *Oar* and *The Parchment Boat*, selections from which are reprinted alongside new poems in this collection. In a piece like 'After the Burial' from *Oar*, the sense of plain reportage enables the poet to go behind the actions described, the ritual burning of a caravan after a death, and towards a moment of clarity about human purpose, 'where reason and civility show their second face'. Conversely, in a poem such as 'Patched Kayak', the almost incantatory effect of apparently simple questions ('Who made the parchment boat?') leads the reader willingly to accept both the strangeness and the rightness of the last lines as applied to the 'making' and the 'wounds', 'which curved along the edges of the lives of seals, / the edges of the lives of women, / the edges of the lives of men.'

In these earlier poems, Cannon shows off the strengths of her poetics, and the reader of her work addresses new poems with a sense of questioning where she might go next. *Carrying the Songs* brings into sharper focus some themes which underlay previous work. Here, ideas of emigration and return, of transformation and endurance, are aired, but this time there is a sense both of a greater political or social urgency, and a distinct unease about what may be lost as language makes its great shifts through history. Several pieces play on the Gaelic and English twinning and untwining of words. The question of the role of language itself as a carrier of the 'songs' of the collection's title becomes central both to the content and the shaping of these poems:

> Our words are cart-ruts
> back into our guttural histories...

begins the poem 'Our Words', where 'Hard slangs of the market-place / are ground down to pillow-talk' and 'The new words are golden, glamorous.' As a poet, however, to enter fully the problem of language itself requires an engagement within the poem at that very moment of its becoming self-conscious; but it's not clear if this poet wants to go there just yet. 'Our Words' ends with a word mill on the ocean floor which 'grinds them out, / keeping the tongue salt.' Such a salve in the final line of a poem, which seeks to air a real poetic issue, might begin to seem habitual and it's true that many pieces do reach toward an upturn of 'vital grace' in their last moments. However, there are poems here which try to address the human quest for meaning – alongside the artistic quest for a lasting artifact – and which attempt to resist that kind of temporary poetic resolution.

'Oughterard Lemons' comes to us with 'A whiff of spice roads'. This, coupled with the use of five verbs with 'had' in as many lines ('had plant-ed', 'had rooted', 'had brought', etc.) might have sufficed as an indicator of what we are then told: 'some dreams sustain us totally, then fail us totally'. However, a measure of the issue this poet is dealing with is to observe how she brings a statement like 'some hardly take at all' to a conclusion that allows a survival 'in the tang of a placename, / in a crazy bush tilted by the wind.'

It is clear that 'the abandonment / of leaven and savour' ('Demolition') is what 'hurts badly', and a reader cannot fail to be implicated in the fears marked out there. The natural world, particularly that of seals, swallows and birds of the sea, is a place this poet returns to often, as if it's there that the issues which animate these poems will find their best rendition. 'Survivors' gathers symbolic meaning from the sea-potatoes, 'pieces of sea-porcelain'. In a moment of loss, adumbrated throughout the collection, the protagonist lifts one 'to admire its pinpoint symmetries / and it falls apart'. However, this poem has the churning tide unexpectedly able to save the sea-potatoes, which though their spines have worn off, are given 'an impossibly safe landing / for frail coats of bone.'

That ending is satisfying in itself and sends this reader back to several other favourite lines – all of them final lines. It seems that in this collection Cannon displays a characteristic movement towards an ending which, for other poets, might be where the poem begins. She leads us, not to epiphany, but to the moment before such a crucial occurrence, as if she is unpacking the building blocks of linguistic and spiritual memory to lay bare how we decide which ones to keep, which to discard. With such a large project, it is not surprising that the plain style of rhythmic spoken speech employed might occasionally feel declamatory. However, in poems such as 'Golden Lane', we are taken in by the hope of 'Today it feels likely', and are willing to enjoy the path to the idea of eternal return and 'a low sun returning.'

Paula Meehan is interested in the moment when our hand in the myth kitty meets something contemporary, harsh and unavoidable. With verve and brio, Meehan can bring together 'toxic algal scum' and 'water / by whose shores Oisín had hunted'. In reading these poems, a sense builds that to be actively present in the physical world may both be part of an aesthetic as well as a kind of prayer or daily practice, something almost Buddhist about its precise intensity.

The motifs of breath and death underpin the overall thrust of this book and the dichotomy that this implies is fully explored in poems such as 'The Following Message Will Be Deleted From Your Mailbox' and 'She didn't know she was dying but the poems did'. In 'Her Void: A Cemetery Poem', Meehan shows why death is one of the poetic subjects that demands its right to enter the poem. Here, in tightly controlled and entirely unsentimental stanzas, she faces the absence that only death creates:

> She'll speak no bitter word, no curse
> or twisted cleverality; no slight, no mean sarcasm
> will riffle the calm pool of her void.

It's typical of Meehan to allow a coined word like 'cleverality' do a lot of the work of implication around how this character lived, how she conducted that act of will which is living. It's rare to see a poet hold up the morgue-mirror to a reader quite so closely: 'a smile – is now a rictus grin'. The transient life brought into relief here is given just a momentary sense that at least life is not death yet, and only at the end are we urged to 'sit and take a breath.'

With these themes in play, it is not surprising that this may be Meehan's most formally experimental collection to date, with several rhymed and unrhymed sonnets as well as poems which rely on the couplet or a shaping stanza, and the unforgettable 'Quitting the Bars', a witty nod to Elizabeth Bishop's villanelle, 'The art of losing isn't hard to master':

> Quitting's hard but staying sober's harder;
> stranger for your being both ward and warder.

Meehan is concerned with the state of 'our primeval bed'. She wants to explore what we hold to be 'good' within the world of our inner lives, that which feeds the spirit, that which engenders poetry. With this poet, a nature poem would have to take account not only of the ecological situation of even the suburban natural world, but also of our tendency to want things from nature that are just not there. She brings these two things up against each other in 'Death of a Field', the opening poem of this book and one which is destined to find its own way as poems of a certain strength and feel for the zeitgeist are wont to do. 'The field itself is lost the morning it becomes a site' is the opening but it soon becomes clear that the 'end of the field is the end of the hidey hole', and:

> The end of thistle is the start of Bounce
> The end of sloe is the start of Oxyaction
> The end of herb robert is the start of Brasso
> The end of eyebright is the start of Persil

But this is not just a litany of loss or even of changes that language can gleefully accommodate. By the end of this poem we have moved to a profound moment of yearning which seeks to possess or be possessed through something larger and all encompassing, 'In every wingbeat in every beat of time.' The strength of 'Death of a Field' is that it does not offer a new pastoral for our time but moves into that mysterious place where poetry carries its own song.

The final section of *Painting Rain* contains a poem called 'Troika' which is, on one level, a searing portrayal of an extended Dublin family, written 'in the light of ancient Greece'. We are warned by the section titles to be aware that it is also a meditation on the act of poetic creation: 'How I Discovered Rhyme' gives way to 'A Reliable Narrative' and 'This Is Not a Confessional Poem'. It is however a poem which, once read, will not be forgotten, and it amplifies the sense of the final section of this book that our endeavour to edify the 'good' – that Greek notion – is key to Meehan's current aesthetic, and this – as with O'Malley and Cannon – is coupled with the sense that archetypal, elemental clashes have always been the stuff of poetry, from suburban Dublin to the western seaboard, and all points in between.

Miriam Gamble

ICONMAKERS AND ICONOCLASTS

Gillian Allnutt, *How the Bicycle Shone: New and Selected Poems* (Bloodaxe Books, 2007), £12.
Janet Frame, *Storms Will Tell: Selected Poems* (Bloodaxe Books, 2008), £12.

The *Collected Poems* are the territory of the connoisseur – one goes to them when one has already been bitten by a poet, and sometimes less for fair reasons than foul (witness Sinéad Morrissey's glee in 'omnivorous *Completes.*/ For their froth. Their spite. For avoidable mistakes'). The *Selected*, on the other hand, is an introductory enterprise that favours 'regulation.../ with everything in that should be in –/ all belted & buttoned & shining'. There should be room for the poems to shine as individual entities, also for a developmental line to make itself felt. So great is the number of poems in Gillian Allnutt's *How the Bicycle Shone* that one can't see the trees for the wood, or the bike for the other bikes. At the risk of a low-brow reference, it's like looking for a distinctive vehicle on the highways of Beijing.

That said, the trees, when they are visible, are frequently worth regarding closely. Allnutt's is a troubled aesthetic, half Beckett and half Thomas à Becket. When she offers clarity, that clarity is hard won and of the most appealing kind – as in 'Sojourn', where it invokes the pared simplicity of haiku, and of Irish and Scottish Gaelic poetry:

> The fettered hill.
> The skull.
> Old stone, among nettles fallen, near.
> Her light brown hair.
> The brief bales.
> The bared hills, the load-bearing hills, the hills of Lammermuir.
> Her coming headlong here.

The evocation of an angular and elemental landscape here is powerful, and strikes with immediate conviction; as with the best haiku, it is simple only on the surface, orchestrating a subtle mediation between the lasting and the transient. Unlike many poets, Allnutt is also able to turn this style towards the town: in 'Clara Street', she paints with a sure hand the 'common language' of the urban neighbourhood without claiming to find a lasting foothold in it:

On the windy street Polly makes her complaint.
I'll miss her

and the hills. I went to them on my bicycle
but they have no thoughts.

And in 'After the Blaydon Races', she gives voice to the epiphany-from-a-hard-place: the vibrant colour of the bus returning from a Saturday day-trip is compared with the cold, fleeting beauty of winter sunlight on the eaves:

Shall the old yellow bus, October, stop and beautifully steep us
in its pennyworth of ale, its picnic

cloth of gold unfolded on the rough grass?

Look how it briskly bowls by the rough sky-grass where houses were
and the forgotten, poor, affectionate people are,

berates us not as does the law in its bald helicopter

There is both relish and *tristia* here: a generosity of linguistic spirit that manages not to overstretch itself, give too much; a will to belong both communally and in the world at large that yet reserves serious doubts about one's right to identify. Allnutt's engagement with the urban is not, as in early Douglas Dunn, the frisson of the poet rubbing against the unwashed masses. Rather, it is something at once purer and wider-reaching (and thus, perhaps, more trustworthy). These poems differ from the landscape poems only by way of locale; the fundamental concern in both cases is with the fragility of human life, and thus of human endeavour and creation. Peter Forbes describes Allnutt as a 'quietly original poet who has followed an uncompromising path': this is true in a number of ways, but most strikingly in the persistent nature of the interest she brings to every surface situation. As with the symbol, the particular circumstance of the poem is always less important for itself than for the something larger it represents and hovers around. Whilst this can (and particularly in a volume of this size) lead to a sense of repetitiveness, it is undeniable that the underlying motif – life as 'sojourning'; poem as temporary stay – is explored and made new in and across an impressive range of territories; indeed, the consistency of her intent is probably behind Allnutt's ability to 'sojourn' with unusual ease. By not 'belonging' anywhere, and making this her theme, she can traverse the ground of both rural and urban traditions; she is also an adept mistress of the historical poem, and a significant reworker of the religious lyric in a predominantly secular field.

Formally, Allnutt tends towards the fragmentary lyric: this is in keeping with her sense – as both religious poet and post-Beckettian writer – of the fundamental inadequacy of language as expressive tool, and also of the hopeless gaps in understanding which the naming of things through language works to cover up. An early poem, 'Blackthorn', describes poems as 'quick black holes', and throughout *How the Bicycle Shone* there is an emphasis on 'the gaps in thought', 'the holes in everything': the failure of the poem to arrive at comprehension (in both senses of the term). This can send the poems awry. Too often, they depend upon the power of the isolated image when the image doesn't have that power – one appreciates the rationale behind the 'unmaking', but every poem cannot get away with being a 'glass bead game', a turning in the palm of clear marbles, then cloudy ones. When it works, however, as in 'The river, Yenisey', 'for laura two weeks old', and in many of the sequences, it works to striking effect, pointing up, respectively, the loss of mystery in the post-religious world;

> Our speech is meaningful, like money.
> We are mute, literate.
> We are in love with our own imagination, the name
>   of the river, Yenisey.
> We know nothing of namelessness, nothing

the fraudulent compression of the unknown into the known;

> [we] have borrowed a name
> for you   a hand me down
>
> who are you   apart
> from laura
>
> the souls of the dead
> inhabit the red bean   said
> the egyptians   darkly

and, finally, the making of a whole picture out of disjointed scenes – ('Sophia', 'A Shepherd's Life'). Allnutt is particularly drawn to the genre of *ekphrasis*, and gravitates always to what has not quite made it onto the canvas, rather than to what has: she is all about probing the spaces between, highlighting the fractures in the narrative. It is perhaps something of a gamble to found an entire aesthetic on this one technique, but when it meets an apt subject, it produces poems at once deft and probing, in which every word and turn is weighed exactly and with consummate skill. At their best, the poems in *How the Bicycle Shone* are confident linguistic depictions of a world in which language and the self are tentative and never at home; they are also as carefully crafted as the religious objects whose genesis Allnutt likes to detail – things painstakingly brought through the alembic to come out the other side 'whole and frail and beautiful as bone/ or prayer,' and sounding the pure sound of the bell.

The pure sound is also a concept much considered in Janet Frame's selected volume *Storms Will Tell* – though here it's less unambiguously welcomed as a certain good. The book combines poems unpublished during the author's lifetime, and subsequently collected as *The Goose Bath* (2006), with a generous selection from *The Pocket Mirror* (1967), the only collection of poems Frame published in a lengthy career as prose fiction and life writer. At her death, hundreds of manuscript versions of poems in various stages of completion were discovered; *The Goose Bath* is the reward of painstaking and careful sifting of those manuscripts by a triad of editors. We should thank them for their effort. *Storms Will Tell* is a positive cornucopia, and contains some of the most exciting poems I have read in years.

Frame, as in every aspect of her life, was a fish out of water in the critical climate to which her earliest poems were subjected. The New Critics counselled for measure, respect for the poem's 'elders'; Frame's poems are more akin to the 'subjective spume' of the radical, the 'quick Caesarian insight' she describes in 'These Poets'. Though she is capable of simple pellucidity – the poem that 'speaks quietly but does not mumble' – her predilection is for the bountiful, the swift, the quirky (and the murky): that which sits in opposition to predictable patterns. Despite her oft-quoted dismay at the imperfections and excesses of her work, there is no space in Frame's poetical world for the artisan:

> Some of my friends are excellent poets
> modestly packed with knowhow, the practising a craft look about them
> in control of their words which in print
> are welldressed in the classical style.

True poetry, 'Some of My Friends Are Excellent Poets' goes on to suggest, 'has not room' for the 'tiptoeing in foot prints already made' implicitly identified as the accepted standard of excellence. Rather, the real work must fight to go its 'own way' – a characterisation which recalls both Heaney's early remarks on his poetry and his later distinction between 'craft' (teachable) and 'technique' (inherent). Frame's poems do occasionally suffer from what Heaney refers to as a 'wobbly craft'; their technique, however, is solid and sure. These are poems which had to be written rather than poems written by someone who wanted to 'be a poet', and they dice with failure as Beckett said art should.

It would, however, be misleading to imply that Frame's poems do not have a relationship with the canon; they jib against the mores of their own time, but embrace a fruitful dialogue, in particular, with the Romantic period. Frame is drawn to the Romantic take on poetry as vision; she is equally well apprised of the complexities at play within that aesthetic, and is never guilty of a simplistic presentation of vision as 'truth'. Rather, she prioritises individual perception, castigating the lazy social processes that work to normalise both language and experience. In 'Hilda', a parable-based style relates the story of a woman who 'stared with uncombed locks of vision / upon a fire that none put out / that no one saw.' The official response is to appropriate and tame that vision:

> So they gave her glasses with deceiving
> lens to try to make her mind
> surrender the insane believing
> that world is fire and men are blind.
>
> [...]
>
> Now Hilda lives as sensibly
> as any woman, and the sun's
> Antarctica as far as she
> is burned by it or strange visions.

Unruly rhythms and half rhymes recall the style of Blake, and the poem's conclusion turns the tables on the purveyors of social grace as wickedly and brilliantly as Blake might himself have done:

> But the retired firemen, their wives and sons
> still grind their bones in bedroom dark
> to try to flint the quenched visions
> of Hilda with her squinted heart.

All our more 'acceptable' impulses, Frame suggests, work towards precisely the transcendence of seeing represented by Hilda, and ironed out by niggardly conventions. Most people can only tolerate a tightly constrained version of 'reality'. To see truly, by contrast, is to accept 'the word-stranger glimpsed out of the corner of the eye / lurking in the wilderness', to embrace contrariety and the inexplicable, however dangerous to one's sense of self that embrasure may be.

This is also the joy and life of language (and the language of life), and something that is paradoxically flattened out by being got to grips with. In 'The Cat Has a Mouthful of Larks', the attraction lies in toying with the unownable thing rather than in final and successful capture (the poem also queries the ethics of 'capture', recognising that language grafts meaning onto things rather than attaining to private 'truths'):

> Not bound to keep an eye
> on almost immobility
> the cat on the mat, a white goddess,
> looks away,
> for unadorned place,
> concealed time
> are not her prey;
> only the thing struggling to get, some time (morning, noon, night)
> to some place (earth, sky, space).

As cat and poet are aligned here, so too the action represents more broadly the nature of human desire (Frame's primary subject), which is always striving for what is out of reach. Desire causes pain, but permits a fuller existence than the easy submission to a recognisable framework. Against those who accept, for example, the underground system as everyday fact (' "Take the escalator," they say'), or who attempt, as in 'The Pocket Mirror', to rationalise into a workable system that which they cannot explain, Frame sides with Bach – the eponymous hero of one of her best poems, 'a musical gossip / writing an aural manual of fucking positions / between man and silence' – and with anything addicted to seeing the world from a number of perspectives. The sun, she remarks, ought to have been awarded 'an Honours Degree in Perspective'; the same might be said of a poet who offers us poems in the voices of, among others, the Guggenheim museum, a person trapped inside an orange, an anemone, a cat, a piano, a brain tumour, language itself.

As there are many different angles from which Frame may see the world, there are also many Janet Frames: *Storms Will Tell* houses a number of excellent political poems (see 'Dunedin Story'); there are also poems which rework the role of the feminine in literature ('The Servant', 'Sweet Corn'), poems about language and poems which invent their own languages, satirical poems, metaphysical poems – the list could go on. Just when you think you have your finger on what she is doing, Frame hits you with something else, then something else again; her canvas is 'incorrigibly plural', and she has the linguistic and stylistic tools to pull this off. Though it may occasionally yearn for the pure aerial vision of the Gods (who eschew the 'infected' vehicle of language), Frame's poetry is ultimately more at home grubbing at the head height of the human, even the child. For adults, 'two or three feet taller,' 'heaven though nearer is further away': ratiocination predominates, and the potential for discovery is dimmed. The child's mind, by contrast, rejects linear argument in favour of a present tense revelling in possibility; its world is spatial, unconcerned with the necessity of turning the logical 'page'.

Janet Frame's poems return the reader to a time before 'the oppression of knowing / surged in us refusing to set us free / from what we had begun to be'; they also redeliver language anew, and make of its status as a medium prone to 'complexity, confusion, fluidity' a bonus not a defect. Reading her, our thoughts suddenly 'glow, are glossed with sun': the ideas are startling, so too the words in which they are delivered.

Kevin Kiely

LONG LIFTED NOTES

Rita Dove, *Sonata Mulattica* (W W Norton, 2009), hb $24.95.
Jean Valentine, *Little Boat* (Wesleyan University Press, 2007), hb $22.95.
W S Merwin, *Selected Poems* (Bloodaxe Books, 2007), £9.95.

George Augustus Polgreen Bridgetower (1780–1860) cuts a dash as violinist extraordinaire through nineteenth-century Europe amidst Haydn and Beethoven in a five-part sequence by Dove, who is daring in this epic poem made up of poems of varying lengths. Her vast historical paradigm has much to depict: 'God's whip lash straight down / the heaving back of England'. It is also metaphysical: 'proof that each of us bears inside / a ruinous, monumental love.' Bridgetower's concert tour is heralded the way John Lennon wrote 'Being For the Benefit of Mr Kite!', which the Beatle 'found' on a poster; hence she uses contemporary journalism in 'The Seaside Concerts': 'the boy is / a former pupil of Haydn, as well as the grandson / of an African prince'. And the wunderkind is also exposed in persona poems, where he raps:

> So let's scrape the catgut clean, stack
> the chords three deep! See, I'm no quack –
> though my only house is on my back.
> All men are beggars, white or black.

Bridgetower, a mulatto, is post-political, he is not not a prototype of W E B Du Bois or Malcolm X, more Nigel Kennedy crossed with the late Michael Jackson, and with no illusions about showbiz ('I am a smudge, / a quenched wick, / a twig shrouded in snow'), where the rise to fame is a never-never land of false promise.

Dove ingeniously manages the required plot: 'Summer ended power-fully – as if God / had snapped a branch from his mightiest oak'. And, protagonists such as Haydn, an establishment figure, is not too happy that the public have a new idol in Bridgetower: 'the daily newspapers thickened / with judgments on the drummed-up duel / between the Maestro and his student of yore.' Shades of Ibsen's *Master Builder*. There has to be sex: erotica, exotica but subtly non-*Kama Sutra,* achieved in 'Seduction Against Exterior Pilaster, Waning Gibbous': 'the humpbacked moon / dumped its rapturous froth / over lawn & balustrade.' Things that go hump in the night. Dove is not a costume drama poet, obviously does not believe in it, or strive for the past as in Pound's *Cathay* or Berryman's 'Homage to Mistress Bradstreet'. This is not literature as museum artifact fakery, instead the dynamic of the silent poetic line as cold as print is musically alive through the language. She does not descend to descriptive passages and deftly brings in European cities:

> London surges, Rome bubbles, Paris promenades;
> Dresden stands rigid, gazes skyward, afraid.
>
> Vienna canters in a slowly tightening spiral.

Beethoven enters the fray while Bridgetower anticipates a life of glory and profits. Poems such as 'First Contact' and 'Augarten, 7 am' reveal how tough it gets trying to crawl up to the top. The sequence becomes a short drama between sections III-IV, showing Bridgetower's chat up lines upstaging a romantic like Beethoven. He can score barmaids but it will be short lived. It is only an ageing boffin like Haydn can truly claim, 'I have starved in these streets with nothing / but a splintered voice / and the angels inside my head'.

As with any creative enterprise, Dove has to find an ending, or as poets say 'an abandoning' of the poem. She takes her cue from the maker of *Citizen Kane*. Welles said, 'If you want a happy ending, that depends, of course, on where your story stops.' Bridgetower is not Paganini, Keats or Modigliani, so a tragic close is not pursued, in that a tragic life in the arts must have a substantial talent or myth behind it. She saves her poem by zooming in on Haydn's head, literally. The lost skull of Haydn makes her point about the artist's immorality. Bridgetower becomes a mere study in contrast and on that reading of this poem, you will have to make up your own mind. Bridgetower is the minor artist through whom the major artists in Dove's tableaux are exposed to their detriment. This is satisfactorially about the arts scene even as Balzac portrayed it, revealed as a shady if not dirty business. She admits, in 'The End, with MapQuest': 'Do I care enough, George Augustus Bridgetower, / to miss you? I don't even know if I really like you.' So Dove as Galatea creates her masculine Pygmalion and wonders if using all that plaster was a waste of studio materials? Yes, and no. Bridgetower is no more than Woody Allen's Zelig, a 'nobody' with a walk-on part in his era, but the irony for Dove seems to be that Haydn's skull is an item of interest, a museum piece, while his art is the immortal part; presumably and in many ways this is the artist's ultimate gamble in life and art. Haydn's skull, incidentally, she tells us, was re-united with its skeleton only in 1954 at Eisenstadt. Come to think of it, Bridgetower too was a much-travelled head in his day. Alas, poor Yorick. Alas, poor Bridgetower. Alas, poor Haydn. One thinks of Robert Emmet, Edmund Burke and Frank Lloyd Wright, who are of unknown final resting place. Bridgetower is buried in Kensal Green, London and has a small plaque to his name. So he made it after all.

A frequent visitor to Ireland, Jean Valentine has, in *Little Boat*, produced a collection reminiscent of Robert Creeley and Cid Corman. There are overt sources in the notes indicating the *Gnostic Gospel of Thomas* and the insight wisdom of Bhanu Kapil Rider; however, scholarly sources never impinge in these miniaturist, crucible poems. Their effects at best implode gently in the mind like a *kōan* after a fruitful period of meditation. Her title comes from *la chalupa*, the drifting boat of the soul, as she implicates Medieval Theology and goes as far back as Aristotle's *De Anima*. There is originality of form and content, meta-linguistics, and metaphysicality. Yet accessibility is her primary aesthetic, so revelatory narcosis is the most you will receive. If you are never going to buy this book, at least get it at a library or borrow it just to open the doors of perception and discover Valentine's inscape and epiphany. Leaving aside her traditional source landscapes, this collection is light as thistledown that blooms in mushroom clouds within the psyche. It is a psychedelic reading experience. Buddhism meets mysticism and various other schools of esotericism, the occult and her Gnostic Jesus as in 'The Woman's Poem', where a mother quotes *St Thomas's Gospel* since mothers are, generally, God to their offspring:

> And now you say
> *Split a piece of wood,*
> *and I am there.*

In 'Annunciation Poem' an infant is present:

> circles dark hair, your fontanel
> – since that second you've been, been the eye of my eye.

Elsewhere, there are vast depths between each word rendering a resplendently spiritual presence through the post-print dreamscape, as in 'The Afterlife Poem', which would have to be quoted in full: perhaps you will read it sometime.

Major life events and changes such as death are calmly transformed: 'Time—you bore it on a green leaf / under the ground.' 'At last' has an epigraph from Blake which is a quiet triumph over death. Quite a claim, eh? In 'The Look' there is a Buddhist affirmation:

> Pain took me, but
> not woke me – no,
> years later, your
> look
> woke me...

This is a poetry of immediacy, her language is explicitly new and beyond simple statements: 'All night long I listened to the coal train'. Wisdom gently creeps out from these poems as their titles draw you into serious matter: '*How will you / have you prepare(d) for your death?*', which concludes in the dying words to the world declared by Jesus and paraphrased by John of the Cross: 'I know you brokenheart before this world, / and I know you after.'

In 'Eye of Water' the language becomes mere sound not sense. 'Moose and calf' takes it impetus from a memory of being on the highway but soon becomes a complexity about pain:

> whose heart in your side is broken in two
> just by a chance comma of time...

The 'comma' is *le mot juste* that is everywhere the tenor of this collection, further exemplified from 'To my soul':

> And what we had
> give way like coffee grains
> brushed across paper...

It echoes with Lawrence's 'The Ship of Death' and has a depth beyond Eliot's 'I have measured out my life with coffee spoons'. Some may clamour at Valentine that poetry should be like stand-up comedy with jerky jokes about conservative politics, should make us laugh all the time, in awe at its rehearsed cleverness. Whereas she is with Plato and the wisdom tradition: philosophy is a preparation for death, and poetry too. Her poetry comes from the myriad mood swings of solitude, written in solitude and for the times of solitude, be they long or short.

One can't help associating W S Merwin with the arresting line, as in Eliot's infamous one about the sky like 'a patient etherised upon a table'. Both poets are poles apart but not in this effect, which Eliot surpassed, while Merwin adopts a muted and occasional startling simplicity. To choose at random in this fulsome *Selected*, from 'Departure's Girlfriend':

> Loneliness leapt in the mirrors, but all week
> I kept them covered like cages.

Or, from 'Provision': 'The dead increase their invisible honey'.

He is only a 'mere' New Yorker by birth, a Princeton college boy praised by Auden and something of an émigré in the American tradition linked to Henry James, Pound, Eliot, and Plath. Captain Bloodaxe here presents a copious assessment anthology of Merwin, showing the poet's deep meditation on death and intense grief but with a steady gaze, a cold Yeatsian eye devoid of luxuriant song. Within the inferno of his work there is nothing creepy or Gothic, nothing Poe-esque: there is control. One of the elegies – more restrained than Hopkins's 'Felix Randal' – is 'The Dry Stone Mason': a fairly devastating performance but again great control in a post-emotional poetry about a sublime visit to a graveyard where one close to the heart lies buried:

> And stones drip where his hands left them
> Leaning slightly inwards
> His thirst is past

'Avoiding News by the River' has the same Merwinnian qualities – post-grief, post-Pantheist and post-Romantic:

> I am not ashamed of the wren's murders
> Nor the badger's dinners
> On which all worldly good depends
> If I were not human I would not be ashamed of anything

In those lines are Merwin's vision: the present poet-reviewer tends to judge poets on their treatment of pain, evil and the sunnier sides of life, amongst other poetic tenets. A typical political poem of the late 1960s is 'Presidents': 'The president of shame has his own flag / the president of lies quotes the voice / of God'. Some retrospective pieces here tend to outshine familiar poems ('The Drunk in the Furnace' and 'For the Anniversary of My Death'), such as 'Berryman', an early mentor of Merwin's, who here is depicted as holding to the tradition and codes of creativity:

> he said the great presence
> that permitted everything and transmuted it
> in poetry was passion
> passion was genius and he praised movement and invention

Another piece in this vein is 'Lament for the Makers', a Who's Who of the poet's life and contacts, from Dylan Thomas to James Merrill and the dreaded dame of American poetry,

> Sylvia Plath then took her own
> direction into the unknown
> > from her last stars and poetry
> > in the house a few blocks from me

His presence in London as his friend passes away is part of this tapestry of *la vie du poète*; the exciting matter for Merwin is that akin to Eliot: poetry is personally unimportant, which is a quality of the post-Ego, a non-concern for posterity, poetry as the preparation for letting go as in 'Cover Note'. Merwin's life voyage can be charted – if you know his work – through this collection, with its Giorgione cover painting, 'The Hour Glass' – irony of ironies, attributed to Giorgione, somewhat like one of those poems attributed to Shakespeare that can't be proved to be of his authorship. Merwin's final *jettatura* here is another irony perhaps, about being bereft of the muse, in 'The Nomad Flute'. He has been a nomad himself, a Ulysses (one of his favourite mythological heroes, mentioned in some poems). Merwin could survive one feels in his present Hawaiian hermitage even without the muse, as a defiant ageing Rimbaud, yet he is still publishing – his Pulitzer Prize-winning *The Shadow of Sirius* is due later this year from Bloodaxe – and is currently a vigorous circuit poet in America: they are rightly proud of him.

THE NOMAD FLUTE

You that sang to me once sing to me now
let me hear your long lifted note
survive with me
the star is fading
I can think farther than that but I forget
do you hear me

do you still hear me
does your air
remember you
oh breath of morning
night song morning song
I have with me
all that I do not know
I have lost none of it

but I know better now
than to ask you
where you learned that music
where any of it came from
once there were lions in China

I will listen until the flute stops
and the light is old again

Peter Sirr

THE METAPHYSICAL TRAMDRIVER: READING LUCIANO ERBA

Luciano Erba, *The Greener Meadow: Selected Poems*, translated by Peter Robinson (Princeton University Press, 2007), $17.95 / £12.50.

The poetry traditions of different cultures intersect quite randomly at the best of times. Poets will, if they can, peer over the fence of language to see what the neighbours are up to, or rely on the services of translators to bring them the news. Sheer happenstance often determines what gets translated: what happens to interest a given translator at a given time, what publisher is prepared to publish the result. Italian poetry has, in fact, been pretty well served in English. Of twentieth-century poets, Montale, Ungaretti, Saba, Pavese, Zanzotto, Bertolucci and Luzi are all available in fine recent translations. Catherine O'Brien's anthology *The Green Flame* is still an excellent starting point for an exploration of contemporary Italian poetry, as is Jamie McKendrick's monolingual Faber anthology, *The Faber Book of 20th-Century Italian Poems*. But the immediately useful context for Luciano Erba is Peter Robinson and Marcus Perryman's translations of Vittorio Sereni published in 2006 by the University of Chicago Press. Indeed Peter Robinson tells us that the first words of Erba's that he read were in a poem by Sereni which cited two lines from his early poem 'Tabula Rasa?'.

Sereni – like Erba a Milanese poet – was one of the most significant figures of post-war Italian poetry and one of the defining poets of the so-called *linea lombarda* or Lombard line, a term originating in an anthology edited by Luciano Anceschi in 1952. The *linea lombarda* is taken to mean a certain kind of lyric sobriety, a poetry of reality, of things, of the quotidian, and often marginal; metropolitan in tone and often subject-matter, anti-idealistic or disenchanted, unillusioned. None of these will apply equally to the various poets associated with it and like all such terms it's more useful as a shorthand than a true analysis. Erba's own view of the usefulness of movements can be gauged from his poem 'Lombard Line':

> Prejudices, commonplaces I adore
> I like to think that there are
> always girls with clogs in Holland
> that they play the mandolin at Naples
> that just a bit anxious you await me
> when I change between Lambrate and Garibaldi.

Lambrate and Garibaldi are train stations in Milan; from the romantic clichés of Holland and Naples to the bathos of the poet changing trains is itself an entirely characteristic journey through shades of irony.

Probably the most defining characteristic of Luciano Erba is detachment – less a political position than a function of his sensibility. Fastidious, delicately ironic, he doesn't fit comfortably into any category. Italian critics have observed the traces of Montale and Sereni but also his distance from the hermeticism of the 1940s, as from post-war neorealism. They cite his 'natural lightness of touch' and preference for highly concrete details, as well as his subtle and apparently even-tempered music. In his introductory essay Robinson emphasises Erba's anomalous position in the post-war context: 'In a cultural context where all is "political", detachment of a French nineteenth-century bohemian kind, of a Gautier or Baudelaire, can be crudely construed as reactionary.'

France and French poetry are important to Erba – he has translated Michaux, Ponge, Reverdy and Blaise Cendrars among others. One of his early poems is dedicated to Philippe Jaccottet who, like Erba, is a highly visual and material poet whose poems are, in his translator Derek Mahon's words, 'recognisably circumstantial, and empirical in their relation to the "real world"'. The earliest poems here display a talent and sensibility already fully formed. Erba strikes his distinctive note and announces the temperament as well as the typical concerns of the work. He seems to have a very secure sense of where he is in relation to the tradition and the contemporary scene – but also he has a clear confidence in his own procedures. Only certain things tempt him into speech and very often they are things which are concealed, submerged, at the margins of experience:

ANOTHER CITY

The vignette in the old illustrated book
never noticed under its tissue paper
all the times I'd turned the pages
revealed to me another city
that climbs and stretches along a river
under a night-blue sky.
From the roofs men look at stars
which seem like kites
women appear on high loggias
while on the far bank of the river
a traveler ties his horse to a tree-trunk:
he too has discovered the city.

A typical Erba poem of this period begins in an offhand manner, and with a few quick brushstrokes blocks in specific details and a mysterious situation.

TABULA RASA?

It's any evening
crossed by half-empty trams
moving to quench their thirst for wind.
You see me advance as you know
in districts without memory?
I've a cream tie, an old
weight of desires
I await only the death
of every thing that had to touch me.

The specific details – the half-empty trams, the cream tie – seem to struggle to press some vivid reality on a scene the poet seems to have half-vanished from. The dandyish tone seems itself to function as a kind of self-removal. The relationship with the world seems to operate within ironising distances. We are always conscious of the poet arranging his composition and placing himself as a self-aware character in his own dramas. Sometimes the poems present themselves as snatches of conversation offered without preamble or context. They are often as much about what is excluded as what is present, relishing their silences as much as their articulations, and the concrete details can be deceptive – they don't so much tie us to a world as signal an attitude; they are knowing, subtle, highly conscious of themselves as artefacts and of their relationship with the tradition. The early poems evoke, or seem to evoke, a world of orderly comfort, of panama hats, fathers in white linen suits, cream ties and elaborate hats and women in fresh blouses:

Your white blouse, Carlina,
who ironed it with such care?
    –'AFTER THE HOLIDAYS'

Or, from 'A First-Degree Equation':

Your latest blouse, Mercedes
of mercerized cotton. . .

It is 'the beautiful country' of memory, all iconic detail sufficient unto itself, the world as a series of meticulous friezes. It's tricky to decipher the precise tone of these poems, and transferring their nuances is probably the single most challenging translation task. Their mixture of irony and longing give them a simultaneous intimacy and distance; their ambition seems to be, as in 'In the Ivory Tower', to 'tell long stories of things / we've to leave behind.' Yet Erba's manner of telling is as much as about concealment and suggestion:

> To tell and describe: medals
> clouds tapestries skies
> ciphers that are born in the hair
> lamed zayin aleph
> to D on June mornings.

The notes inform us that 'D' is a person and that the hair falling across her forehead somehow evoked the Hebrew letters. It's a signal, maybe, that telling and describing function as elements in a highly individual erotics of perception.

Peter Robinson includes an essay by Erba at the end of the book, 'On Tradition and Discovery', which emphasises his distance from the various established modes of thinking about poetry and 'isms' in general, and argues for 'authentic simplicity' and the 'importance of *objects*':

> Whether you're dealing with enlarged details, or with Gulliverised scales, even if we'd better not speak of gracious miniatures. I recover in this way the vision of adolescence, at least so I believe. It is in the comparison with the little, in the discovery of what had always escaped the attention, that I encounter the most diverse and unexpected surprises of being. Attention is always altered, conditioned by intentionality; by nature it misses the mysterious. I prefer the deserts of inattention, the haystack, not the needle.'

It may well be that Erba's is 'a poetry of objects', as Robinson notes in his translator's preface, and that 'Like other Milanese poets with whom he is associated, he avoids the dangers of high afflatus in the Italian language...by sticking to the details of circumstantial existence'; but it is the manner in which the objects and the circumstances are disposed that really defines the poetry, and the apparent materiality can be as much a hindrance as a benefit for the translator. The objects and the poetry exist in a mind space that is both very distinctive and deeply embedded in the Italian poetic tradition, and the particular weight of the objects or poems can be hard to gauge. And it is a poetry 'that lives in its intimate expressive detail'. The brevity and lightness of the poems also pose their own challenges: 'The translator has such a small canvas on which to effect an equivalent coordination of parts, and to find a recognisably similar lyrical gesture as that performed by the poem itself.'

There is, though, a temperamental affinity between Erba's mandarin modesty and the expressive range of English. The English poems which Robinson has made out of Erba's originals sit well in the tradition of English-language poetry. The 'lyrical gesture' of the Italian seems to work as efficiently and as tellingly in English. This may be due to the tonal range Erba deploys; he is as much a poet of tone as of objects, and to enjoy him you have to tune in to his particular range. Once attuned, there's much to enjoy. Some of the earlier poems here are as fine as anything he later achieved. One of the most striking is 'Senza Risposta' ('Without Reply') a love poem or doubt poem, questioning yet still cool and poised:

> Ti ha portata novembre. Quanti mesi
> dell'anno durerà la dolceamara
> vicenda di due sguardi, di due voci?

> November has brought you. How many months
> of the year will the bitter-sweet
> affair of two looks, of two voices endure?

In the original the repetition of the idea of the woman 'portata da novembre' has a powerful rhetorical effect maybe not quite replicated in English:

> ...non sono
> che un uomo tra mille e centomila
> ma non sei
> che una donna portata da novembre
> e un mese dona e un altro ci saccheggia.

> ...I'm only
> a man among thousands and hundreds of thousands
> but you're only
> a woman that November brings
> and one month grants and another plunders from us.

Poems like these don't seek any other purpose than themselves, and they resist definitive closure. They find their urgency in a kind of spareness and wit. The expedition of 'Book of Hours' ends with a separation in the city 'amid building-site quartz and mica' ; the poet and his companion return home 'pursued at our heels by life / as by a friendly dog that catches up with us.'

These early poems were written in the 1950s, a period of much experimentation in Italian poetry. Seventeen years separate the publication of *Il male minore* (*The Lesser Evil*) and his next collection, *Il prato più verde* (*The Greener Meadow*), so it may well be that Erba felt himself very much out of step with the poetic currents of his era – that he was too Frenchified, too middle-class, too much the self-aware ironiser.

In 'On Tradition and Discovery' he also affirms his attraction to 'indefinite space', 'undecided regions, uncertain places, non-places'. Something in Erba's imagination comes alive in these interstitial regions. In 'Closing a Trunk Once More' an unused object, a hat found in a trunk and replaced once more, is the impetus. The poet is literally suspended between the worlds of earth and sky in 'I Live Thirty Metres From the Ground', where he imagines what happened in the air he now occupies:

> crossed over centuries back
> perhaps by a flight of herons
> with below it all the falconry
> of the Torrianis, the Erbas even
> and fine horses on the margins of ponds.

The in-betweenness is also a reflection of the middle-class identification most explicitly portrayed in 'Without A Compass':

> According to Darwin I'd not be of the fittest
> according to Malthus not even born
> according to Lombroso I'll end bad anyway
> and not to mention Marx, me, *petit bourgeois*
> running for it...

Robinson comments acutely on how a poem like this 'outflanks the sorts of class-based political criticism that Erba's work had received at the hands of Franco Fortini and others. Yet, nevertheless, *"petit bourgeois"* is exactly the experience with which Erba's poetry might fictively identify itself, because that is a class in ambivalent transit between two more unequivocally valorised social positions.' It's certainly true that Erba returns again and again to emblems of bourgeois life – the obsessive attentiveness to clothing, the expensive 'raphael album' in which his 'blondest daughter' draws, or the fine furniture in 'Relocation' which offers a solitary consolation to the relocated gazer. When the rest of the city moves for the bars on a foggy evening:

> you head for the foggy blue sign
> of a furniture shop display
> where you look at the damask beds
> the pettineuses the buffé the contrabuffé
> then go home and stand a long time at the mirror.

It's an equivocal poetry, a poetry of indefiniteness which holds the world at bay, and yet paradoxically this allows the world to press itself all the more powerfully on his senses when he does admit it. Some of the finest of the poems from the 1977 collection *Il prato più verde* (*The Greener Meadow*) are the poems written for his daughters, including that collection's title poem, where all of the details combine to a form a kind of incantatory naming, as if the act of naming, of marshalling the evidence of the real could amount to a spell against disenchantment or metaphysical despair.

There are several other poems in this vein, such as 'The Goodbyes', and 'Seven and a Half', all economic and controlled gestures making much of the most unexpected and unpromising materials, and all seeming to observe life from a bemused height, finding their energy in the zone between belief and disbelief. Maybe his most characteristic poem is 'The Metaphysical Tramdriver' from his 1989 collection *L'ippopotamo* (*The Hippopotamus*):

> Sometimes the dream returns where it happens
> I'm maneuvering a tram without rails
> through fields of potatoes and green figs
> the wheels don't sink in the crops
> I avoid bird-scarers and huts
> go to meet September, towards October
> the passengers are my own dead.
> At waking there comes back the ancient doubt
> if this life weren't a chance event
> and our own just a poor monologue
> of homemade questions and answers.
> I believe, don't believe, when believing I'd like
> to take to the beyond with me a bit of the here
> even the scar that marks my leg
> and keeps me company.
> Sure, and so? another voice *in excelsis*
> appears to say.
> Another?

This 'Credo, non credo' defines very well the Erba enterprise, a scepticism which secures itself in the tangible – though it's entirely typical that for Erba the tangible should be represented by a companionable scar.

The translations are very close to the originals and often deliberately flat – as if the intent is to move them as little as possible into an English-language comfort zone. They very much defer to the originals on the left-hand pages, and probably assume the readers will direct themselves to those. This might explain a certain awkwardness of phrasing sometimes where the English leans a bit too heavily on the Italian and the transition from poem in Italian to poem in English doesn't fully come off. In this sense the best way to enjoy this selection is stereophonically, moving from the Italian to the English and back again. This closeness is Robinson's stated aim in his 'Translator's Preface': 'I prefer translations that stick as close to their originals as possible, but which nevertheless aim to read as poems in their new language.' More often than not he succeeds very well in finding an 'equivalent gesture' in English for what Erba does in his own language. He gives us a body of intriguing and challenging work that adds considerably to our sense of the tonal range of post-war Italian poetry.

Liam Carson

A BURNING HYMN

Edited by Michael Almereyda, *Night Wraps the Sky: Writings by and about Mayakovsky* (Farrar, Straus and Giroux, 2008), hb $27.
Ariadna Efron, edited and translated by Diane Nemec Ignashev, *No Love without Poetry: The Memoirs of Marina Tsvetaeva's Daughter* (Northwestern University Press, 2009), hb $24.95.
Marina Tsvetaeva, translated by Elaine Feinstein, *Bride of Ice: New Selected Poems* (Carcanet, 2009), £14.95.

'The might of my voice shakes up the world', declaimed Vladimir Mayakovsky in his poem 'A Cloud in Pants', as translated by Matvei Yankelevich. If there is any image that springs to mind of Mayakovsky, it is of the poet as revolutionary ranter. In *Night Wraps the Sky: Writings by and about Mayakovsky*, edited by film director Michael Almereyda, Val Vinokur compares Mayakovsky to rapper Emimen: 'the two share not only a grandiose and overexposed lyrical sensibility but also a relentlessly mechanical style'. Almereyda speaks of Mayakovsky's 'proto-punk ferocity'. In his memoir 'On the Captain's Bridge', written in 1940, Lev Kassil delivers a hilarious account of a Mayakovsky 'reading' in which the audience egg on the poet as he verbally demolishes hecklers; they 'clap, stamp, shout, cheer'. At one point he is asked: 'Mayakovsky, with what part of you do you think you're a poet of the revolution?'. To which he replies: 'In the place diametrically opposite to where that question was born'.

Mayakovsky saw himself as a 'present-day Zarathustra' preaching Marxism ('I may simply be / the thirteenth apostle / in the most ordinary of gospels'). In an essentially post-communist world, with its awareness of Soviet horrors – Stalin's Terror, the Gulag, the genocide of the kulaks, the stifling of all political opposition, not to mention a fundamental crushing of individual artistic expression – it is easy to forget the thrill that Bolshevism held for a poet in 1920s Russia.

To read Mayakovsky and to read about him is to be reminded that the Soviet Union was once regarded as 'the most tremendous government experiment ever conducted'. It's also worth noting that the birth of communism dove-tailed with the rise of potent new technologies. Both promised rapid change, the demolition of old ways. Almereyda places Mayakovsky within the context of Futurism, as a man 'enraptured by city life, by machine-age energy and speed'. Mayakovsky wrote of 'our new souls – / humming / like the arcs of streetlights.'

'The revolution was a psychological imperative,' Patricia Blake writes, '[Mayakovsky] was a born rebel. It was in his temperament. At the same time, he was alienated... I would say that much of his life was spent in the search for refuge from this pain that hounded him, and he sought it in the absolutes of his time: the revolution, communism, and, when they failed him, in death.'

Like Marina Tsvetaeva, Mayakovsky committed suicide, putting a bullet through his head in 1930, at the age of thirty-six. Perhaps he could no longer live with the tensions between the political and the personal, the collective and the individual. For all his extolling of a communal socialist Utopia, Mayakovsky's poetry was, like Whitman's, a song of the self. He wrote 'I am where pain is – / everywhere' (translation by Max Hayward and George Reavey). And as the Soviet state laid waste to Orthodox churches, it's curious to note Mayakovsky's frequently Biblical turn of phrase, wherein he speaks of 'the thorny crown of revolutions'; 'my Golgothas in the halls of Petrograd, Moscow, Odessa, and Kiev'; 'we ourselves are creators / within a burning hymn' (translations by Max Hayward and George Reavey).

In his essay 'Mayakovsky: His Language and His Death', John Berger deals with the vexed question of translating Russian poetry. His belief is that Mayakovsky has become reduced to a 'romantic political legend rather than...a poet' because of the difficulty of rendering his work into English. In nineteenth-century Russia, the distinction between written and spoken language was not as marked as in Western Europe. Berger contends that 'it was not mere personal arrogance which made Mayakovsky believe that he could speak with the voice of Russia'. In Russia, much poetry is widely known by heart, primarily because Russian lends itself to rich rhyming and rhythmical effects. Sound and rhythm were central, and Mayakovsky himself wrote of this in 'How Are Verses Made?':

> Rhythm is the fundamental force, the fundamental energy of verse. You can't explain it, you can only talk about it as you do about magnetism and electricity.

It is rhythm which bubbles throughout Mayakovsky's verse, and which drives it along 'with an assaultive energy in every taut or terraced line'. The Hayward and Reavey versions in *Vladimir Mayakovsky: The Bedbug and Selected Poetry*, edited by Patricia Blake, tend to replicate the visual form of the original Russian, with their long lines and staggered cascading breaks. Their versions are radically different to those in *Night Wraps the Sky*. The following is one example, the Hayward and Reavey translation followed by Ron Padgett's from *Night Wraps the Sky*:

Men of posterity

          examine the flotsam of dictionaries:

Out of Lethe

      will bob up

          the debris of such words

as 'prostitution,'

      'tuberculosis,'

        'blockade'

And:

So go look them up

   in your dictionary:

      jackoff

      mutation

      underground.

To be fair, the Padgett version is described as an 'adaptation', but it is an extreme case of how utterly divergent takes on Mayakovsky in English can be. One really does yearn to have an understanding of the original Russian.

Night Wraps the Sky has a clear agenda, to introduce Mayakovsky to a new audience. Thus we get versions that utilise a modern idiom for Mayakovsky. So, in the two versions compared above, the poem title that Hayward and Reavey have as 'At the Top of My Voice' becomes Padgett's altogether catchier 'Screaming My Head Off'.

Night Wraps the Sky, though, is not just about Mayakovsky the poet, but also the 'orator, playwright, magazine editor, stage and film actor, poster maker, jingle writer'. It's a generously illustrated and exquisitely designed book, with archive photographs, cartoons, posters and photo-montages. Mayakovsky once wrote, 'In the poet's wake, thousands of street folk: students, prostitutes, salesmen', and one of the most affecting photographs is of the tens of thousands at his funeral procession. *Night Wraps the Sky* is, in many ways, an excellent introduction to Mayakovsky, but its lack of any bibliography, index or suggestions for further reading is disappointing. I personally would have liked to have read more of Mayakovsky's undoubted influence on Allen Ginsberg and Frank O'Hara. These flaws aside, this book is a reminder of Mayakovsky's enduring spirit.

In Ariadna Efron's *No Love Without Poetry: The Memoirs of Marina Tsvetaeva's Daughter*, edited and translated by Diane Nemec Ignashev, one comes across uncanny echoes of Mayakovsky's approach to language. Efron tells us Tsvetaeva 'would mumble to herself, testing words for their sound'; 'she read poetry aloud in a voice not for the salon but for the concert hall'. In *Marina Tsvetaeva: The Double Beat of Heaven and Hell*, Lily Feiler speaks of their 'similarity of temperament…in their poems of love and loneliness, each echoed the other'.

For Efron, the October Revolution propelled the language of the street and the village on to a greater stage; poets were presented with 'heretofore unheard words'. She speaks of Russia and the Russian language '[taking] root in [Tsvetaeva] with all its multi- and polyvocalism, with all the national character of its dialects, sayings, and vernacular, with all its songs of glory, all its funeral laments, potions for the evil eye, and other sorcery'.

No Love Without Poetry frequently makes heart-breaking reading, not least in Ariadna's descriptions of her 'profoundly conflicted and profoundly lonely' father Sergei Efron:

> Perverted notions of comradeship and fidelity to one's oath, combined
> with growing awareness of the doom awaiting the 'White' movement
> and the impossibility of betraying the doomed, led Sergei down the
> most mournful, erroneous, and thorn-laden path in the world, through
> Gallipoli and Constantinople, to Czechoslovakia and France, into the
> ranks of living shadows, of people without citizenship or nationality,
> without present or future, with the unbearable burden of having only
> the past behind them.

Efron also recounts Sergei listening to Tsvetaeva reciting her paean to the White Army, *The Demesne of the Swans*, with 'great suffering in those huge eyes of his, before announcing 'it wasn't at all like that, Marinochka'.

If Sergei Efron was a haunted figure, so was Tsvetaeva, and Ariadna includes a precocious and telling portrait of her mother, written when she was only seven:

> She is sad, quick, and likes Poetry and Music. She writes poetry. She is
> patient and tolerant to an extreme. She can be angry, and she can be
> loving… Sometimes she walks around as if lost, then suddenly she
> seems to awaken, begins to speak, and then drifts off somewhere again.

In exile from Russia, both Tsvetaeva and Efron were lost figures. Of her mother, Ariadna observes: 'Through cities and suburbs – I speak not of the Russia she left behind – Marina passed *incognito*, like Twain's pauper prince, unrecognised and unacknowledged'. She quotes from Efron's diaries: 'I am not doing well in Prague. I live here as if in a bell jar… And I am terribly drawn to Russia. I never thought the Russian in me was so strong.'

What lingers over much of *No Love without Poetry* is the unsaid, the unspoken. Ignashev addresses this in her introduction, telling us 'one senses everywhere the censorship Efron imposed on herself.' Of her own sixteen-year banishment to the Gulag, her mother's suicide and the execution of her father, Efron mentions little; there are brief mentions of the death of her sister Irina. But these have been documented in harrowing detail elsewhere, not least in Irma Kudrova's *The Death of a Poet: The Last Days of Marina Tsvetaeva*.

Efron concludes with her receiving notice in 1956 from the Military Collegium of the Supreme Court of her father's posthumous rehabilitation. She tells us that since the deaths of her parents, 'I have stopped living and lost all sense of time.' Her memoir is the work of a delicate and skilled writer. It plunges into a past before the darkness descended, brilliantly recreating a childhood world (often with great humour), and takes us into what Ignashev describes as 'the luminous, magical fantasy world of her mother's poetry'. It is also a lyrical portrait of her parents that is profoundly loving. Her final quote from her mother's work is apposite:

> Thus we sink into the night,
> Cradlemates together.

Elaine Feinstein's *Marina Tsvetaeva: Selected Poems*, first published in 1971, was, for many readers, their first introduction to Tsvetaeva's edgy, fiery poetry. It is noted for its fine versions of the Moscow and Blok poems, including a beautiful 'hand is pale from holy kisses'. It has now been updated, expanded, and re-titled *Bride of Ice: New Selected Poems*. To the original collection is added 'Girlfriend', written for Tsvetaeva's lover Sofia Parnok; the fairytale of 'On a Red Horse'; 'New Year's Greetings', written on the news of Rilke's death; and previously missing material from 'Wires' and 'Poem of the End'. It's a disappointment that there is so little new material after so many years. Although Feinstein's versions of Tsvetaeva take their base from literals provided by ten translators, by and large there is a consistency of tone, opting for what sounds natural in English. Feinstein herself admits this can negate Tsvetaeva's abruptness in Russian. Comparing the different versions of 'New Year's Greetings' by Feinstein, David McDuff and Nina Kossman, is a bewildering process. Where McDuff has 'sonorous, stentorian', Kossman has 'hollow, resonant', Feinstein has 'clamorous and empty'.

A comparison of Feinstein's and Kossman's versions of 'I opened my veins' (rendered as 'My veins slashed open' by Kossman) shows stark variations in register or tone. Kossman relies heavily on assonance and an emphatic rhythmic drive; Feinstein's version is altogether more calm, even prosaic:

My veins slashed open: unrestrained,
Unrestorable, my life gushes forth.
Hold steady your plates and your bowls!
                    (Kossman)

I opened my veins.   Unstoppably
Life spurts out with no remedy.
Now I set our bowls and plates.
                    (Feinstein)

It's also worth noting that Tsvetaeva's 'We shall not escape Hell' has
been rendered into Irish at least twice – Nuala Ní Dhomnaill's 'Táimid
damanta, a dheirféaracha' and Celia de Fréine's 'a dheirfiúracha dílse'. Ní
Dhomhnaill wildly riffs on the original, unleashing a flood-tide of images,
and as one reads the poem, it begs to be heard aloud, such is the force of
its alliterative effects and sustained drive. De Fréine's version is more
sparse, but none the less effective for that, touching on the poem's odd
fusion of resignation, revolt and repressed energy being unleashed 'sna
hoícheanta gan suan'.

It is a shame that much of Tsvetaeva's work remains unavailable in
English. Her collection of essays on poetry, *Art in the Light of Conscience*,
has been out of print for years. Many of her individual collections have
yet to be translated in their entirety, and there is no collected edition of
her work in English. It is heartening, though, to hear that Belinda Cooke
– whose *Paths of the Beggar Woman: The Selected Poems of Marina Tsvetaeva*
appeared in 2008 from Worple Press – is working on *After Russia*.

Each translator has his or her merits and flaws. Lines are rendered in
different order, the styles of punctuation used to mimic Tsvetaeva's
rhythmic dramatism vary. Ultimately, though, Tsvetaeva shines through
no matter what – her intensity of expression, her sparkling folkloric and
mythic themes, her ability to sing. She wrote of herself as a 'person
skinned alive...and under the skin – living flesh or fire: me, Psyche'. Of
the many versions of 'Poem of the Mountain', I'm most taken by Nina
Kossman's:

I cannot, now or ever,
Stop up this black hole.
Let me sing of my mourning
Atop the mountain.

David Cameron

THE SHOCK OF THE TRUE

Seán Haldane, *Always Two: Collected Poems 1966–2009* (Greenwich Exchange, 2009), £15.99.

Who is Seán Haldane? Like another poet with the initials S H, he grew up in Northern Ireland, but unlike that poet he left before the Troubles started. He spent much of his adult life in Canada, and now lives in London working as a neuropsychologist with the NHS. In comparison with his near-contemporaries Heaney and Mahon, Haldane is an obscure unknown. For readers who like to make their own discoveries, so much the better: his newly published collected poems, *Always Two*, won't disappoint.

Nor will it take them long to get the measure of the poet or the man. Just two poems in and the distinctive Haldanian voice and character assert themselves. The early poem 'The Bullhead' describes – rather, enacts – the poet's youthful rage at his girl's unfaithfulness:

> Next day we crossed by boat to Inishmore,
> She gaily singing to the other men,
> And when we climbed to Dun Aengus fort
> I muttered to myself I'd smash her head
> On the sharp teeth of the chevaux-de-frise:
> Each spike of stone went straight into my heart.

Here, clearly, is a poet unconcerned with showing himself in a good light. That sexual jealousy can spill over into violence – even if only fantasised violence – is an unpalatable truth that this poet of love will not simply airbrush out of the picture. Indeed, the book's short, fascinating foreword quotes Montale on the 'would-be poet' who 'only looks for that part of himself which is the most acceptable to others'. The point would be lost were either Haldane or Montale merely out to poke fun at bourgeois sensitivities. Haldane is nothing if not civilised. His dismay at the barbarity which engulfed the North for three decades is seldom voiced in these intimate poems; but when it is, Haldane doesn't waste his time divining the motives of the barbarians themselves. In 'My Father, St Mark's, Armagh', he asks:

> Could you have heard the shot
> When a man – some violent thick,
> Who knows? – was rendered not?

If the plain-speaking is characteristic here, then so is the honest doubt of 'Who knows?'. This sometime 'lecturer, part-time farmer, small press publisher, and psychotherapist' knows much, but doesn't pretend to know more than he knows. His love poetry displays scrupulous psychological realism rather than mysticism. Take another early poem, 'Midwinter Racing'. This starts with the metaphor of lovemaking as skiing, but by the third verse the poet really is skiing, and we realise that the metaphor occurred to him because skiing is such a natural part of his life, part of this particular day that begins with lovemaking.

To describe Haldane as a poet of love might seem limiting, even harmful to his reputation. After all, Robert Graves's star has waned in recent decades, at least among literary critics. And there is a link between these two poets. Those who have found a way to Haldane's poetry might well have done so via Martin Seymour-Smith's biography of Graves, in which the elder poet is quoted as saying that, as Oxford Professor of Poetry, he 'met two or three undergraduates who had something *to* them'. Seymour-Smith adds: 'One of those was the poet Seán Haldane, whose work Graves always admired.' Coming from a man who was notoriously critical of fellow poets (refusing to keep a book of Auden's on his shelves: 'bad for the soul'), this is not nothing.

Graves was a master poet, but his love poems tend to revolve around the brilliant beginning or else (with greater realism) the sour ending of romantic love. Nothing wrong with that: a poet takes his inspiration where he finds it. An anthology of great poetry descriptive of love's long middle part would be pocketbook-size. But this is where Haldane excels. There are a half-dozen lovers' (or spouses') dialogue poems at the heart of this book which are beautiful, true – and painful too. 'Butterflies' ends:

> 'I'm not in love with you.
> When I feel butterflies
> In my stomach the way I used to do,
> I'll let you know.'

> 'Is there no in between "in love / attached"?
> Can't you just say you love me?
> I love you. Sometimes I'm in love with you.'

> 'I'm not in love with you.'

If Haldane is not a 'love poet' in any limiting sense, one quality he does share with such poets through the ages is a ravishing lyrical power – which he is content to withhold from the reader when occasion demands. Unlike Graves, Haldane is scientifically trained, and uses the language and thought-processes of science even in the context of love, unselfconsciously and not always ironically. Here is the non-scientific (but lyrical and plain) first verse of 'Honesty':

> The parchment panes of honesty
> Reflect the candle-light.
> I want to make a vow
> To be as straight in future
> As I am, naked, now.

And this is from the last verse of 'Zero':

> The membrane of so-called zero
> Holds tubules, vesicles in plasm
> Moiled on each other oiled by flow,
> Cyclosis of the jism, and spasm...

It is to Haldane's credit that he is capable of both these styles, but there is little doubt which is the more moving.

A complex love poet, Haldane also (as 'Honesty' shows) writes exquisite nature poems – that other staple of the English poetic canon. 'Fritillaries', for instance, is a lyrical poem about flowers – and also about physical longing, remembered passion, feeling 'an old ache'. It's a poem about more than flowers but the flowers in it are never less than real. The poem sways with the life in them.

The key to understanding this poet is provided in the foreword: 'I don't trust a poem,' Haldane writes, 'unless it is written straight out in a state of something like shock – the shock of what feels like truth.' Whether or not this is an approach to poetry you approve of, one benefit it confers on this book is the complete absence of the usual dull stuff that would-be poets routinely (and some real poets occasionally) indulge in. Gerard Manley Hopkins criticised Wordsworth for being 'too essentially Wordsworthian', which might sound perverse, or just funny, like Bob Dylan's remark that Adolf Hitler had a Hitler moustache. But you can see what Hopkins meant. He is talking about inspired writing where the actual level of inspiration is not sufficient to take the poet out of himself, beyond his customary way of looking at things.

As astonishingly varied as Haldane's poems undoubtedly are, they display specific characteristics, a consistent voice, which mark them out as written by Seán Haldane and no other. They are 'Haldanian', but not 'too essentially' so. Haldane is very far from the impersonality advocated by Eliot. If he is angry, he lets that anger show; in surveying past relation-ships, he doesn't pretend to a magnanimity he doesn't feel. These are poems originating in the unconscious of a man who wants to live as consciously as possible. Their author can appear determined and wilful in them, but the poems themselves are not willed into existence.

'Black Hill' is one poem in which Haldane's will seems to be overthrown by a female – this time a girl encountered on a walk across moorland, though she is under the ground, 'blue eyes scrunched narrow', telling him that she was killed with her mother and father, that 'Death is more than you want to know', and instructing him:

> Draw me a circle on the stone
> With your finger, a cross in the circle – so.
> And put your lips to the circle – so.
> This is my forehead, kiss my forehead
> So I can feel that I'm not dead.

'Black Hill' is one of a kind – as so many of Haldane's best poems are. This is, to say the least, unusual: when a poet hits a rich vein of form, the temptation is to mine it dry. But there is only one 'The Hugger Mugger' – a truly terrifying poem; only one 'Desire in Belfast', an erotic litany of places in that divided city; only one long fantastical-satirical poem, 'In Gratitude to the General', prompted, perhaps, by the poet's mixed feelings about Wilhelm Reich, whose brand of psychoanalysis influenced his own work in that field.

Perhaps it is Haldane's focus on *sexual* love that keeps him from delving too often into childhood. A beautiful exception is 'What Women Do', in which he describes his 13-year-old self seeing a young Austrian girl at the opera. A prelude to the magnificent 'Desire in Belfast', this less ambitiously moving poem ends:

> Sweet Suzanne of the serious eyes,
> Do you remember me when you hear
> *Cosi fan tutte*? So all women do –
> And all men too:
> We disappear.

This is sad, but oddly consoling. 'What does not die in us is not alive', Haldane writes in 'Night Thoughts', a sentiment expressed in negatives but wholly life-affirming. These poems are very much alive. Read them.

Joseph Woods

THE SOUL OF WIT

Samuel Menashe, *New and Selected Poems*, edited by Christopher Ricks, with *Life is Immense: Visiting Samuel Menashe*, a film on DVD by Pamela Robertson-Pearse (Bloodaxe Books, 2009), £12.

Any review of Samuel Menashe's poetry seems to require the mandatory mention of his marginality or neglect, which goes as far back, at least, to Stephen Spender, who in favourably reviewing Menashe's work – alongside Ted Hughes's *Crow* – in *The New York Review* in 1971, implored that Menashe should be more widely known.

The publication of this book, with an accompanying DVD filmed by Pamela Robertson-Pearse in which Menashe is filmed in his 'cold-water' flat in New York, neatly book-ends the fact that Menashe as an American poet was first published in the UK, and should go some way to enhancing and promulgating his reputation. Indeed, his reputation and visibility have undergone a steady renaissance: *Collected Poems* appeared in 1986 in the US, and that same year a selection of his poems under the prestigious 'Penguin Modern Series' imprint was published in the UK; two *New and Selected Poems* appeared in 2000 and 2005 respectively; and in 2004 he won the inaugural Poetry Foundation's Neglected Masters Award. He has not been short of advocates, as testified to by the excellent introduction here from Christopher Ricks, and additional notices from Donald Davie and Spender, while in Ireland his work has attracted the attention of Austin Clarke and Derek Mahon. Dana Gioia in an earlier introduction noted: 'It is futile to lament Menashe's marginality. One notes the injustice and moves on. Better to celebrate the occasion at hand.'

Samuel Menashe was born in New York City in 1925, the son of immigrant and persecuted Russian Jews. His parents were literate in at least three languages, and Menashe admits Yiddish was his mother tongue by a hair, then English, French and later Spanish. During the war he served in the US infantry; he was one of only six in a company of 190 men who had not been killed, wounded or taken prisoner. After active service, he studied at the Sorbonne in Paris. There he wrote an acclaimed doctoral thesis, an examination of the awareness – religious or mystical – which is the source of poetry, entitled *Un essai sur l'expérience poétique (étude introspective)* and based on a total assent to Baudelaire's dictum: 'In certain supernatural states of the soul the most ordinary scene becomes its own symbol.' It is striking how this notion has informed Menashe's work. He returned to the US where he soon resigned his formal teaching job and,

except for frequent trips to Europe, he has lived in the same apartment in
New York for more than fifty years.

AT A STANDSTILL

That stance, that cast
Of my solitude
Has found its niche
In this kitchen
Where I do not eat
Where the bathtub stands
Upon cat feet –
I did not advance
I cannot retreat

This handsome book is a modest enough offering in the sense that a life's
work is presented in less than 200 pages and none of these poems are
forty-line page-fillers, averaging at four to six lines per poem, and short
lines at that. Here's a second, entire (untitled) poem:

Pity us
By the sea
On the sands
So briefly

This has a Newtonian ring to it – an earlier version of the same poem
avoided left-sided capitalisation, which might better suit the sense of
utterance in these short lines. In reading Menashe you notice this kind of
thing, there's an enormous attention to the tiniest details. Traditional
rhyming matters to him, he has observed that: 'There is a lot of rhyme,
unnoticed, in ordinary speech'. And because his syntax is steady and
clear he mostly dispenses with standard punctuation, it simply isn't
required. Other poems are even shorter at two lines:

The sea staves
Concave waves

He is clearly a miniaturist, and his fidelity to the short form has been
consistent from the outset, and while it's impossible (through his
rhyming) not to be reminded of Dickinson and of the haiku form, he
does something altogether different. Aligning the animate with the inanimate, the visible with the invisible, the Hebrew and Christian traditions,
literary language and the colloquial, he's obsessed with latent meanings

in everyday speech and idiom. Poems beginning with lines such as 'I stood my ground', 'At death's door', 'No more than that', 'You had your say', take on a new meaning when broken down and enunciated syllable by syllable, there is a sense of discovery or renewal as he revives hackneyed phrases. It's worth viewing how he recites entirely from memory on the DVD, aided and abetted by his careful rhyme schemes. While he claims in the introduction that he is not a confessional poet, many of his poems begin in the first person, or are presided over by a first person but veer towards the universal. A number have something of the Anglo-Saxon riddler about them, to the extent that you'd almost expect a key at the back of the book.

In terms of literary influences, Menashe's only direct declaration was made in his second collection, *No Jerusalem But This*: 'I believe in the Prophets and Blake'. This is the Blake of *Songs of Innocence* and *The Everlasting Gospel*, and together with the English translation of the Hebrew Bible, they are his sacred texts, mimicking Blake's declaration that all he knew was in the Bible and that 'the Old and New Testaments are the Great Codes of Art'.

The Old Testament prefigures what will be interpreted, and perhaps this throws some light on Menashe's poems, they are not reactive, the event occurs before the cause. Apart from Blake, the only other poet who matters to Menashe is Hopkins, many of whose poems he knows by heart. These influences ensure that Menashe's landscape is essentially a biblical one.

MY MOTHER'S GRAVE

Bones
Are mortar
For your wall

Jerusalem

Dust
Upholds
Your street

In this poem, Jerusalem acts as a conduit between personal grief and the larger grief of civilisation in dust. It is biblical with its iconography of proud cities in devastation, of palaces overgrown, and is reminiscent of vignettes from the Greek Anthology or even Paul Celan. In the poem, 'Paschal Wilderness' –

Blue funnels the sun
Each unhewn stone
Every derelict stem
Engenders Jerusalem

– the elements conspire to create a concept of the imagination, begetting
one's own Jerusalem; the word 'derelict' unhinges the pastoral and
intimates the possible fall. Menashe's landscape is the declarative
landscape of sacred history, miracle and epiphany. His perception of the
physical world is often eclipsed by the inspiration of it as sacred:

The hill I see
Every day
Is holy

Other poems allude to Adam, 'I am the man / Whose name is mud'.
Bread is also perceived as symbol with its ancient significances. A poem
entitled 'Manna' is supported by a passage from Deuteronomy. The poem
'Daily Bread',

I knead the dough
Whose oven you stoke
We consume each loaf
Wrapped in smoke

can be read as domestic harmony until we read 'dough' as the slang for
money and along with 'consume' we are suddenly 'wrapped' not so much
in the mystical ecstasy of smoke but more the smoke of domestic strife.

Samuel Menashe claims that from an early age it was the piercing
economy of the poetry and narratives of the Bible that ensured his interest,
and so – along with Blake – David, Isaiah and Solomon can be enlisted
among his sacred poets. Like the passage from Kings (19:11-12) that
Menashe has cited as influential, his is 'a still small voice' but a significant
one, his poems are alternately joyous and elegiac, freighted with history
and tradition and yet inhabiting a space between the literary and the conversational. His concentration on brevity of form has not prevented him
from contemplating the universal; like his mentor Blake, Menashe too
can see the world in a grain of sand.

Nessa O'Mahony

SEED AND BREED

Edited by Joan McBreen, *The Watchful Heart: A New Generation of Irish Poets* (Salmon Poetry, 2009), €18.

Joan McBreen performed a major service to Irish poetry when she brought together the work of 113 Irish women poets in her 1999 anthology, *The White Page* (Salmon Poetry). That book sought to correct the imbalance in the representation of women writers in Irish poetry anthologies and proved in the process that Irish women's poetry was vibrant and diverse. As a poet included in that anthology, I turned to McBreen's latest collation with anticipation and curiosity; given the slew of anthologies of Irish poetry over the past few years (for example, Bloodaxe's *The New Irish Poets*), I was intrigued to see what rationale she might use for her latest choice.

The Watchful Heart contains the work of twenty-four poets who represent, for McBreen, the new generation of Irish poetry. Each was born in the last fifty years, has published at least two collections of poetry and wasn't featured in *The White Page*. Each poet has also contributed three poems, along with an essay in which they explore an issue close to their hearts as poets. The editor points out that had she also drawn on the poets contained in *The White Page*, she would have produced a volume far larger than either she, or her publisher, intended. So here we find ten women and fourteen men, representing what McBreen terms 'some of what I felt would be the best of recent Irish poetry'. She makes no claims that her selection is either 'comprehensive' or 'all-inclusive', a statement that rather dilutes the fun for the reviewer, of course. How can one possibly rant away about the exclusion of Mr X or Ms Y in the face of such reasonableness?

Of course, the question of what makes a 'new generation' is relative. I turned to the book expecting new faces and comparatively recent publication histories; imagine my surprise, therefore, to discover editor, publisher, anthologist and teacher Pat Boran as the first poet featured. Surprise mingled with pleasure, of course; Boran's lambent poetry has delighted me for a long time and, as a poet who began writing in the 1990s, when Pat was a regular teacher of creative writing workshops throughout the country (not to mention the author of one of the best creative writing handbooks produced in Ireland), I have always seen him as a wise mentor of an earlier generation. But he's actually only a year older than me and, in terms of chronology (he was born in 1963), he fits the book's criteria. Indeed, his inclusion serves as a timely reminder of how much he has managed to achieve in a comparatively short time-period and he is, as I said, always a pleasure to read. This splendid haiku, dedicated to the poet Leland Bardwell, proves the point:

A housefly settles
on the still end of my pen:
haiku counterweight.

Clearly an ageist approach isn't going to elucidate McBreen's method so suffice to say that established names, for example Peter Sirr, John O'Donnell, Leontia Flynn and David Wheatley, mingle with poets whose reputations deserve to be far more widely known. Mary Branley, whose essay coincidentally also evokes the spirit of Leland Bardwell, has three fine poems here. I particularly liked the skilful rhythm of 'Sé do bheatha a Mhuire', where the lilt of the prayer's lines is artfully captured:

lift and drop
atá lán de ghrásta

rattle and whist
of the *máidí raimhe*

It's also nice to find Patrick Chapman here, another admirably prolific writer of poetry, short stories and screenplays. Chapman can range from mordant humour to lyric romanticism; we get both in the first poem in his selection, 'The Darwin Vampires', where the eponymous villains are shown both in 'those places in between, where microbial kingdoms, / Overthrown with a pessary, render needle-toothed / Injuries invisible', and in 'A taste-regret on someone's tongue; a sudden tinted / Droplet in the iris of a fading smile; a blush upon / a woman's rose'. Chapman's essay, in fact a series of Fortune Cookie aphorisms, kept me giggling; I particularly liked the notion that 'Your ancestors will not be proud of your work, because they are dead.'

Two Irish-language poets are featured, Louis de Paor and Gearóid Mac Lochlainn, each with poetry in the original and in translation. Louis de Paor's accompanying essay is a thoughtful meditation on the advantages and limitations of translation which, he points out, is necessary. 'The original remains obstinately, shyly, out of reach, and yet the impression it leaves on the linguistic veil that both conceals and reveals confirms the marvellous diversity of languages other than our own.' Mac Lochlainn explores the issue creatively; his poem 'Aistriúcháin Eile', rendered as 'Translation', suggests the slippery, protean quality of the task:

Is shín Barra amach a lámha láidre,
is síos leo láithreach san fharraige sáite,
gur thóg amach bradán beo beathach,
bradán ársa na beatha.

Then Barra stooped and thrust his hands into the sea
And pulled out an ancient fish
That kicked and writhed against his grip,
And showered them both
In glitters of water.

Nuala Ní Chonchúir is another poet who writes with equal fluency in Irish and English, as her most recent poetry collection, *Tattoo: Tatú* (Arlen House, 2007), revealed. But here she is purely in English-language mode, and demonstrates her characteristically sharp eye for a killer image, as in the poem 'Foetal', where 'we are fastened to our bed / you curl to the curl of me / unshaped to a shape that fits'. She also demonstrates the carefully thought-out nature of her poetics in her essay on poetry as 'female self-portrait', where she claims literary descent from writers such as Eavan Boland, Sharon Olds and Edna O'Brien. Cherry Smyth is equally articulate on her process. For Smyth, writers are 'designed to speak, to tell stories and when the listener and we get lost in the telling, the story becomes an art.' Her art is clearly visible in poems such as 'December Morning, 2007', where:

Dying is always happening,
holding up its dark mountain
from the depths of a lake,
questioning the summer table
on the winter deck, the unplanted earth.

Not surprisingly in this increasingly mobile age, the 'new generation' features some poets who no longer claim Ireland as their home. John McAuliffe settled in the UK some time ago, although his poetic imagination seems equally at home in his new locale and in the childhood home of memory. I particularly liked the sense in the poem 'A Midgie' of the poet making matter out of his immediate surroundings: 'The garden goes greener in the lilac time. / This will go down on the permanent record'. Mary O'Donoghue is also based abroad – she lives in Boston – but finds an entire world as her point of reference. In an extract from her 'Letters to Emily: Finding Your Voice' she writes:

a shriek to make Atlantic waves turn tail,
turn a church on tiptoe on its steeple,

a shriek so pure and true it's heard
at the bottom of an Australian well,

as if the London air raid warning
was sounded by a pipistrelle...

In his essay, Justin Quinn uses his vantage point as a resident of Prague to examine the changes that have occurred in Irish society and wonders whether 'a fundamentally new immigration pattern...can...invigorate the monoculture that has held sway since 1922.' Provocatively, he adds that 'there's a corresponding ambition that the category of "Irish Poetry" itself will go up in a puff of smoke. No decent poet would ever wish to be merely an "Irish" poet (just as he or she wouldn't want to be merely an American or Australian poet).' Interesting, then, that one of his featured poems, 'The Crease', seems to evoke that well-known poetic stance, that of the wistful emigrant, albeit with a wry tone:

What's the river doing now? Does it blaze
with stunning blue and pink? Does it amaze
next to no-one with its smart remarks
on quays for long-gone merchants and their clerks,
on lopsided buses leaning in on it,
or cranes that raise the skyline bit by bit...

I promised earlier that I wouldn't be one of those reviewers that berates an anthology for its omissions. Each editor is entitled to their choice, for poetry is a subjective business. I did rather wonder why there was no place for Leanne O'Sullivan here (perhaps her fine second collection *Cailleach: The Hag of Beara*, from Bloodaxe, came too late to make her eligible), but I was delighted to read other fine poets, such as Paul Perry, Kevin Higgins, Anne Fitzgerald, Mary Montague, Alan Gillis, Joseph Woods, Damian Smyth, Eileen Sheehan and Kate Newmann. There are many others – Dave Lordan, Ann Leahy, Ciaran Berry and Nell Regan to name a few – who have made impressive débuts over the last decade and who will surely appear in future anthologies. *The Watchful Heart* may not be the last word on Irish poetry at the start of the twenty-first century, but it provides a pretty good taster.

Mary Shine Thompson

REVILING 'VILLAFIED FASHION': AUSTIN CLARKE'S *COLLECTED POEMS*

Austin Clarke, *Collected Poems*, edited by R Dardis Clarke (Carcanet Press / The Bridge Press, 2009), £17.95 / $21.60.

At least one full generation has grown up since Austin Clarke's collected poems were published in the year he died, 1974, in Dolmen Press editions that quickly vanished into the bookshelves of poets and collectors. In the meantime, the deadening vice-grip of the prescribed Leaving Certificate poetry programme crushed the life from lovely poems like 'The Lost Heifer' for that same generation. Hugh Maxton revived interest in Clarke when he edited and annotated a selection of the poems for Penguin in 1991, but a *Selected* of its nature lacks the comprehensiveness necessary for a full reappraisal. Now Dardis Clarke revises the Dolmen edition with the intention of correcting its errors, completing the author's notes and ordering the poems chronologically according to the dates of the original collections.

Here, then, at last, is the *Collected,* all 572 pages that constitute an – almost – entire life's work. (Clarke was unhappy with one poem, *The Sword of the West* [1921], and suppressed it). The book is long overdue and warmly welcomed – not least for the reasons that Christopher Ricks adduces in his elegant introduction. Ricks directs us to Clarke's virtuosity, to the way his intricate rhyming and assonance haunt the ear and the eye, defying closure. His Clarke is an intrepid, honourable escapologist, a man who made his freedom out of his chains. However, Clarke is also one of those writers so tuned to the public pulse that their lives both embody and interrogate the norms of a nation. He is the most *situated* of poets. The chapters of his life story uncannily parallel or comment upon the Ireland of his time, and his poetry recognises, resists and comments upon key public events.

On Easter Monday 1916, Clarke was a bystander during the Rising in Dublin's O'Connell Street, but within a year he had published the first of three epics that form a coded response to the executions of his mentor Thomas MacDonagh and the other insurgents. Those epics may not have had the verve or the control of W B Yeats's verse, but then, Clarke was a twenty-one year old apprentice in 1917 and Yeats a 'great-rooted blossomer' when he changed utterly the rebels of 1916 and found in them a 'terrible beauty'.

In his early twenties, a deep psychic disturbance put Clarke in Swift's St Patrick's Hospital, where his sleep was haunted by the ambient violence of the War of Independence. A half-century later, in the midst of the celebrations of the 1916 Rising, he transformed and calmed that personal hydra into *Mnemosyne Lay in Dust*, a meticulously disciplined and frank long poem on his breakdown, which confidently refined and adapted the American confessional mode.

But that was in the future. Clarke's verse début, an epic entitled *The Vengeance of Fionn* (1917), which was warmly praised by AE, was followed by two further epics, *The Fires of Baäl* (1921) and *The Sword of the West* (1921). Clarke's contemporary critical essays suggest that his intention was to create an elemental landscape in which heroic figures could play out impersonal, racial dramas, thereby promoting a national ideal of stability and order. Thus he could insert himself into an already established poetic tradition which laid claims to timelessness, and write the final chapter in the story of the Irish nation proposed by nineteenth-century historians and cultural revivalists.

The literature of 1916 is, of course, awash with the rhetoric of sacrifice, and it informs the choice of the pursuit of Diarmuid and Grainne as subject matter for *The Vengeance of Fionn*. Clarke's Grainne epitomises the sovereign myth, and the landscape she embodies is a place where elemental, impersonal passions might be possible. Significantly, however, the epic's heroes, Diarmuid and Fionn, are less than heroic. Diarmuid desires death, and Fionn is murderous and petty. To the narrator of the poem, Grainne offers oblivion by way of the obliteration of personal autonomy. Only the poets and bards who play supporting roles in the epic possess the capacity to transcend the aura of gloom with which Clarke invests the poem. Failure and regret also dominate *The Fires of Baäl*, a poem that deals with the events leading to the death of Moses. The promised land is elusive and 'tremendous forces of doom' are everywhere. There is neither consolation nor hope for the future to be found in this poem. Clarke called his third and least successful epic, *The Sword of the West*, a 'horrible untidy room'. There is no centre in it to hold its wild imaginings. Only when he follows his lyrical bent and allows it to overcome his Miltonic aspirations does he come into his own: as in, for example, the plangent 'O Love, there is no beauty, / No sorrowful beauty, but I have seen; / There is no island that has gathered sound / Into dim stone from many reeded waters / But we have known.' In such moments from the extended verse paragraph 'O Love, There is No Beauty', culled from the discarded *Sword of the West*, may be found something of the passion of 'The Straying Student', or of the tenderness of love poems like 'The Planter's Daughter' or 'Nunc Dimittis', which reads: 'It is her lovely voice, I / Hold, whenever we part, / Sharing one breath, silenced / By lips that dare not part.' Ironically, George Russell's kindly encouragement was Clarke's early undoing: it propelled him towards the epic, but the form was a dead end.

And yet – and yet – in this period of unprecedented turmoil at home and abroad, Clarke not infrequently succeeded in evoking a terrifying sense of cosmic chaos and estrangement, of what T S Eliot called 'the immense panorama of futility and anarchy' that constituted contemporary history. The disembodied voices in the epics, their pervasive pessimism, even their structural and narrative discordances, all found their emotional correlative in the War of Independence, in the executions, in the horrors of the World War and its aftermath. Personally and poetically, Clarke was caught up in all these currents. The poems are escapist in one of the senses that Ricks defined: they seek distraction from what normally has to be endured. In their attempt to evade the misery of the present moment they succeed in transposing it into the upheaval and restlessness associated with modernity. Even the epics are insistently 'in history', to use a term Donald Davie applied to Clarke's more documentary mid-century poems. Early and late, Clarke saw the literary value of discordance. In a letter to the English poet Herbert Palmer he defended this tendency, asserting that the outward form of a poem should convey conflict. The fragmenting epics, in the modernist ambition of their 'dying fall' and even in their formal failure, are a record of their age and contain the seeds of Clarke's later prosody.

By the time the new Irish state was declared in 1922, Clarke had a brief marriage behind him, had lost his position as lecturer in the National University and had been forced take the boat to England to find work. There, he says, 'The nightingales / Naturalised my own vexation' ('The Loss of Strength'). There too he re-energised a Celtic-Romanesque utopia that had suffered from literary overexposure in the previous century, remastering it with cold and brilliant colours. His much-quoted note on assonance (that 'takes the clapper from the bell of rhyme...'), to be found in *Pilgrimage and Other Poems* (1929), was written while in England. The asceticism of this book's freshly imagined 'blessed place' exists in tension with an eroticism disciplined by poetic forms. Among the collection's love poems are the memorable 'The Planter's Daughter', 'The Young Woman of Beare' and 'Aisling (At morning from the coldness of Mount Brandon)'. The austerity and sensuality in *Pilgrimage and Other Poems* combine to create a set of rigorous norms against which the clichéd nationalism and piety of contemporary society could be tested and then found wanting.

With the Second World War threatening Britain, Clarke and his young family returned to Ireland in 1937, to live in a house willed (by his mother) on his death to a religious order ('Usufruct'), just as the Irish constitution, that guarantee of democracy and fundamental rights, was being framed. His resistance to institutional religion, and his private life – which included a separation and a second relationship – left him vulnerable socially. Joseph Holloway's comment in 1941, that Clarke's and Denis Johnston's private lives would debar them from accepting the position of director of the Abbey Theatre, suggests something of the climate of disapproval and conformism.

The eleven poems of *Night and Morning* (1938) together reveal a changed man. They are imbued not with the desire for erasure that marked the epics, or the romantic dreaming of *Pilgrimage*, but with a chill, psychic realism. In 'Tenebrae' Clarke confronts the inescapable fact that 'An open mind disturbs the soul', and announces despairingly: 'And there is nothing left to sing'. The dominant tone is self-reflexive. Scarred by the ignorance that had replaced reason and logic, the speaker finds himself 'Too frantic in my superstition'. Selfhood is hard won in a struggle with guilt and shame. It is a selfhood that takes no comfort in the caul of religion – or indeed, in the cultural isolationism that had buoyed Clarke in his twenties. Samuel Beckett's accusation that Clarke's 'deeper need' was a 'flight from self-awareness', finds its riposte in the sceptical urbanity of *Night and Morning*. The collection probes the psychological depths and complexity of a tortured inner self, all the while recognising its inherent dignity. The verse of *Ancient Lights* and later collections, much of which rails against the plight of the powerless, is predicated upon the dignity of vulnerable individuality. It is no coincidence that the defenceless, complex, simple woman, Martha Blake, who needs the miracle of Mass to begin each common day, makes the first of two appearances in this book.

Clarke published no poetry collections between 1938 and 1955 but he was hardly silent. He did publish verse plays and channelled his energies into verse theatre in an attempt to revive and revise Yeats's theatre, building on the surge of interest in the form abroad. Gordon Bottomley's dictum, 'The sound of poetry is part of its meaning', was the motto emblazoned on Clarke's Lyric Theatre programmes, and it emphasised what he saw as poetry's intrinsically oral quality, whether declamatory, conversational, rhetorical, or – as in the case of his poetry programmes that Raidió Éireann broadcast for over a quarter century – didactic.

Theatrical misfortune turned to advantage when the Abbey Theatre burned down in 1952: left without a stage, he abandoned verse theatre and returned to verse itself, finding his inspiration in the world around him. From the mid-1950s he adopted the role of relentless Job, lashing out at local greed and the abuse of power, especially that of the Catholic Church that became 'too great a vine'. What the Irish 'Ill-fare State' ('The Subjection of Women', 'In O'Connell Street') succeeded in ignoring and concealing for decades was writ large in the torrent of coruscating satires in *Ancient Lights* (1955) and after. The state's shameful secrets were there in plain view, in uncompromising detail. Poems addressed the plight of unmarried mothers; physical abuse in schools; animal welfare; homelessness; emigration; ignorant sectarianism; criminal neglect of and cruelty to children; grasping property developers; self-serving politicians: the whole sorry litany of public shame. His verdict was that 'We destroy / Families, bereave the unemployed. / Pity and love are beyond our buoys' ('A Simple Tale').

Denis Donoghue berated Clarke for being perilously close to a 'local complainer'. Clarke never defended himself against the charge: indeed, Donoghue lobbed Clarke's own term back at him. However, the poet-historian escapes the accusation of provincialism because of his use of terrifyingly accurate and concrete local detail, and the accumulation of evidence that incontrovertibly confirms power's capacity to corrupt. Why did no one listen to his angry refrains, beaten into careful form? Why did no one respond when he lashed out at 'Air-scrooging builders, men who buy and sell fast. / One Gallagher bought the estate. Now concrete-mixers / Vomit new villas' ('Cypress Grove'). Or when he reviled new churches 'ugly as sin' ('The New Cathedral in Galway')? Few escaped his vitriol. In 'Burial of an Irish President,' he condemned the pusillanimity of Taoiseach John A Costello, his cabinet and the other dignitaries who would not risk the wrath of Rome to attend a Protestant obsequy. The reference to 'hee-haw' in 'At the Dáil' was a Molotov cocktail shied at Charles J Haughey. Minister for Health Dessie O'Malley was excoriated because he 'glibs our hysteria' ('In O'Connell Street'). In 'New Liberty Hall', a poem on Ireland's then tallest building and headquarters of the ITGWU, the country's largest union, Clarke exposed trade unions' self-importance with the withering comment: 'Labour is now accustomed / To higher living.' He tore aside the veil of mid-century silence to reveal how rights of way are 'Outlawed by greed' ('Right of Way'), and how criminal child abusers enjoyed immunity from prosecution: 'No prosecu-tion / Dare wall our young from persecution' ('Corporal Punishment'). The seven woods made famous by Yeats were 'sold for a song' by the forestry department, and the wily entrepreneur responsible named: 'Malachi Bourke... pulled down / For copper, lead and slate, / A house still remembered abroad' ('The Stump').

With savage Swiftian indignation, sad lives are accorded a dignity in verse denied them in life: the lives of women like Miss Marnell, a convert to Catholicism, or 'Miss Rosanna Ford', who died 'Because she had no shilling for the gas, / Blue-handed, freezing'. Also, the lives of children: 'Three Poems about Children' does not spare the Poor Clare community whose neglect caused the death of thirty-five children (not sixty, as Clarke claimed). A government tribunal of enquiry did, however, exoner-ate the nuns. Clarke insists that we confront what was another open secret: the slave labour that religious orders exacted from 'unmarried mothers'. Always he insists on the sheer physicality of human existence, whether in the sensuous lingering over Mabel Kelly or Peggy Browne in his 'Eighteenth Century Harp Songs'; in the need for family planning; or in the forensic, unsparing detail of the painful decline of 'Martha Blake at Fifty-One'.

With old age came not serenity but outrageous and serious roguery, especially on sexual matters. Clarke conducted his own Irish literary oldster Woodstock Festival: make love, not war, he proclaimed, in long, loping alexandrines occasionally prodded with a walking stick. The sexual antics of Ovid's Tiresias and of the mediaeval Celtic Mis have the capacity to heal in these late poems, but Maxton is surely right when he suggests that the focus on sexual energy suggests a deeper interest in transformation. Clarke's strength was his insistence on naming reality, whether psychological, mental or social, in uncompromisingly objective, tangible terms; and then allowing his metaphoric mind to move on its silent recesses. To the end he held to a doctrine of salvation and of poetry that is grounded in physical reality and in the capacity to transform that reality.

Clarke is a poets' poet who makes few concessions to his readers. He is a classicist and formalist for whom form and erudition are essential to the making of meaning. They enable him to write with 'Invisible ink' as he says in 'The Jest', and thereby facilitate a frankness, especially on sexual matters, that would not have been tolerated in other forms of discourse. He also demands a knowledge of local context complicated by the passage of time. It would not have been necessary in 1968 to explain the identity of Dracunculus to anyone who had read the poem entitled 'Drumcondra'; no one would have needed to be told where the palace of John Charles McQuaid, Archbishop of Dublin, was. The church liturgy informing the poem 'Tenebrae' is now probably unfamiliar to a secular readership. Not every scholar will know now what a 'skyte' is, although every Dubliner certainly will ('More Extracts from a Diary of Dreams').

Clarke's peccadilloes are well documented. Among them are his tendency occasionally to strain after rhyme riche or homonyms; his intermittent, wilful obscurity; and his tenacious experiments with Irish-language poetic modes. His literary virtues and vices equally suggest modernist, rather than traditionalist or even postmodernist principles. Clarke is acutely self-reflexive, and propels language beyond dry land. He also accords writers a signal importance in effecting change. His satires are predicated upon a belief in an ideal world and they equally celebrate and bewail our frightful fall from it. Although he lived through less mythological times than the old artificer Yeats, it is not difficult to discern their shared convictions; and therein lies the basis of their mutual distrust.

At its best – and there is much in that category – Clarke's poetry keeps technique in its rightful place, enabling readers to 'glide between the shades / Of meaning' ('More Extracts...'). Had his verse been limited to a scattering of poems – 'The Straying Student', 'The Scholar', 'Ancient Lights', 'Mnemosyne Lay in Dust' and 'Forget Me Not', say – his reputation would have been secure. But his poetry is not thus limited. This Carcanet / The Bridge Press edition may ensure that at last Clarke, like the midges of Templeogue Bridge, has his 'own enormous day, / Unswallowed' ('Usufruct').

Notes on Contributors

Fergus Allen's first three collections were published by Faber and Faber; his most recent, *Gas Light & Coke*, was published by Dedalus Press in 2006. He has recently recorded a number of his poems for the UK's Poetry Archive.

Ralph Black's recent poems have appeared mainly in American journals: *The Gettysburg Review, The Southern Review* and *The Massachusetts Review*, among others. His most recent collection is a chapbook: *The Apple Psalms*. He teaches at the State University of New York, near Rochester.

Colm Breathnach has published six collections of poetry and his selected poems in Irish *Rogha Dánta* 1991 – 2006 came out in 2008. His first long prose work *Con Trick 'An Bhalla Bháin'* was published by Cló Iar-Chonnachta in September 2009.

David Cameron's stories were published in 2000 under the title *Rousseau Moon*. A poetry collection, *All I Saw*, is forthcoming.

Siobhán Campbell's collection *Cross-Talk* is just published by Seren. This follows *That Water Speaks in Tongues* (Templar Poetry, 2008) which was shortlisted for the Michael Marks Poetry Award. She works as Course Director of the MFA in Creative Writing, Kingston University, London.

Peter Carpenter's fifth collection, *After the Goldrush* (Nine Arches Press), follows *Catch* (Shoestring Press) and *The Black-Out Book* (Arc Publications). He contributed to Iain Sinclair's *London: City of Disappearances* (Hamish Hamilton, 2006) and *La Isla Tuerta: 49 poetas británicos, 1946–2006* (Lumen/ Random House, 2009). He is a Visiting Fellow at the University of Warwick.

Liam Carson is the director of the IMRAM Irish Language Literature Festival, and a publicist with publishing house Cois Life. His reviews, articles and essays have appeared in *Fortnight, The Irish Review, New Hibernia Review, Comhar* and the *Irish Examiner*.

Neil Curry lives in the English Lake District. His *Other Rooms: New & Selected Poems* was published by Enitharmon Press in 2007.

Susan Donnelly is the author of three poetry collections: the Morse Prize-winning *Eve Names the Animals, Transit* and *Capture the Flag* (Iris Press, 2001). Her poetry has appeared in *The New Yorker, The Atlantic Monthly, Ploughshares, Poetry* and many other journals and anthologies. She lives, writes and teaches poetry in Cambridge, Massachusetts.

Bob Dylan released his first album, *Bob Dylan*, in 1962. His thirty-third studio album is *Together Through Life* (Colombia Records, 2009). *Christmas in the Heart*, an album of seasonal favourites, will be released later this year (all proceeds to charitable organisations inside and outside the USA).

Carrie Etter's second collection, *Divining for Starters*, will be published by Shearsman Books in 2011. She has lectured in creative writing at Bath Spa University since 2004 and reviews regularly for the *Times Literary Supplement*.

Diane Fahey has published eight poetry collections and a verse novel. A *New & Selected Poems* will be published by Puncher & Wattmann in 2010. She lives in a coastal town in south-east Australia.

Tom French has published two collections, *Touching the Bones* (2001) and *The Fire Step* (2009), both from Gallery Books. He received bursaries in literature from An Chomhairle Ealaíon / The Arts Council, Ireland in 1999 and 2009.

Miriam Gamble teaches creative writing at Queen's University, Belfast. Her first collection, *The Squirrels are Dead*, is due from Bloodaxe Books in 2010.

Kevin Graham will be published later this year in *The Stinging Fly*. He lives and works in Dublin.

Paul Grattan's first collection, *The End of Napoleon's Nose*, was published by Edinburgh Review in 2002. His work has appeared in the anthologies, *The New Irish Poets*, *Magnetic North* and *The New North*. He is currently researching a Ph.D on the work of the Scottish Poet and cultural thinker Kenneth White. His second collection, *Daytime Astronomy*, is forthcoming.

Daniel Hardisty studied English at the University of East Anglia from 1996 to 2000. His poems have appeared in magazines and anthologies in the UK and Ireland, and he is currently working on his first collection.

Simon Haworth is from Greater Manchester and is completing a Ph.D in Creative Writing at the University of Manchester. Most recently his poems appeared in *The Wolf* magazine and he has also published reviews in *Irish Studies Review* and *The Manchester Review*.

Rita Ann Higgins has published eight collections of poetry, including *Sunny Side Plucked* (Bloodaxe Books, 1996), a Poetry Book Society recommendation, and *Throw in the Vowels: New and Selected Poems* (Bloodaxe Books, 2005). She was Green Honours Professor at Texas Christian University in 2000 and an honorary fellow at Hong Kong Baptist University in 2006. She is a member of Aosdána.

Maria Johnston teaches in the School of English, Trinity College Dublin and at the Mater Dei Institute.

Kevin Kiely is a former Fulbright scholar. Recent publications include *Breakfast with Sylvia* from Lagan Press, and the essay 'A Mystical Element in the Pisan Cantos', published in *Ezra Pound, Language and Persona* (University of Genoa Press, 2008), edited by Massimo Bacigalupo and William Pratt.

Zoë Landale has published six books, including poetry, fiction and creative nonfiction; her latest, *Once a Murderer* (poetry), was published by Wolsak and Wynn in 2008. In 2010, a book she co-edited, *Slice Me Some Truth*, will be published by Wolsak and Wynn. She teaches creative writing at Kwantlen Polytechnic University in Vancouver, BC.

George McWhirter grew up between the Shankill Road in Belfast and Carnalea on Belfast Lough. His translation of Homero Aridjis's *Poemas Solares* will be published by City Lights in 2010. As Vancouver's first Poet Laureate, 2007–2009, his project anthology, *A Verse Map Of Vancouver* (Anvil Press, 2009) featured maps and photographs by Derek von Essen.

Jim Maguire's poems have won a number of prizes, including the Brendan Kennelly Award and the inaugural Padraic Fallon Award. His collection of short fiction, *Quiet People: Korean Stories,* was published by Lapwing in 2008.

Rebecca O'Connor was awarded the 2004 Geoffrey Dearmer Prize. She was a writer-in-residence at the Wordsworth Trust in 2005, and an award-winner in the inaugural New Writing Ventures Poetry Award. Her work has appeared in the *Guardian*, *Poetry Review*, *The Spectator* and *Stand*. A pamphlet entitled *Poems* was published in 2006. She lives in Cavan.

Nessa O'Mahony is currently Artist in Residence at the John Hume Institute for Global Irish Studies, University College, Dublin. Her most recent book is *In Sight of Home* (Salmon Poetry, 2009) a verse novel.

Peter Robinson's *The Look of Goodbye: Poems* 2001–2006 was published by Shearsman Books, who also brought out his *Spirits of the Stair: Selected Aphorisms* in 2009. *The Greener Meadow: Selected Poems of Luciano Erba* (Princeton University Press, 2007) won the John Florio Prize in 2008.

Gabriel Rosenstock is a poet and haikuist, author/translator of over 100 books, mostly in Irish. Cambridge Scholars Publishing recently brought out his twin-volume musings on haiku as a way of life, *Haiku Enlightenment* and *Haiku, the Gentle Art of Disappearing*. Salmon Poetry has just published his début volume in English, *Uttering Her Name*.

Jason Ranon Uri Rotstein is Poetry Editor of the *Jewish Quarterly*. His publication credits include *PN Review, Salmagundi, Literary Review of Canada, Stand, Poetry Wales, Poetry International* and *Maisonneuve*, among others.

Anamaría Crowe Serrano's debut collection *Femispheres* was published in 2008 by Shearsman Books.

Rosie Shepperd is working on an M.Phil at Glamorgan University in Wales, and has had work accepted by *Magma, Rialto, Smiths Knoll, Poetry Wales* and *THE SHOp*. In 2008 she was shortlisted for the Manchester Poetry Prize, and is a former winner of the Ted Walters Prize (University of Liverpool).

Peter Sirr is a freelance writer and translator. His latest collection, *The Thing Is*, was published this year by Gallery Books. His other collections include *Marginal Zones* (1984), *The Ledger of Fruitful Exchange* (1995) and *Selected Poems 1982–2004* (2004), all from Gallery Books. He is a member of Aosdána.

Lisa Steppe has published one collection of poetry in English, *When the Wheathorses Die* (Summer Palace Press, 2001). Her book *Island* has just been published in German (Niebank-Rusch-Verlag, Bremen). She was a winner of the Féile Filíochta International Poetry Competition and was shortlisted for the Strokestown International Poetry Prize.

Mary Shine Thompson is Chair of Poetry Ireland and Dean of Research and Humanities at St Patrick's College, Drumcondra (a College of Dublin City University).

Róisín Tierney's work has appeared in a variety of outlets, including the New Irish Writers page of *The Sunday Tribune, Magma, Arabesque Review* and *The Wolf*. She was one of the readers in the 2008 Poetry Ireland Introductions Series. Her poem *Gothic*, published in this issue, won joint second prize in the 2007 Brendan Kennelly Poetry Competition.

Bill Tinley published his first collection, *Grace* (New Island), in 2001. *Mindent Akarás*, a selection of his work translated into Hungarian, appeared in 2007.

Mick Wood is a theatre practitioner based in Strasbourg. His poems have appeared in *Poetry Ireland Review, Poetry London, Seam, The Interpreter's House, Acumen* and *The Frogmore Papers*. A runner-up for the Strokestown International Poetry Prize, 2006, he is currently working on a first collection.

Joseph Woods is a poet and Director of Poetry Ireland.